SHOOTING IRON HORSES

PHOTOGRAPHING YOUR MODEL RAILROAD

J. Norman Reid

Jeffrey J. Fleisher

Cobbler Mountain Press

Delaplane, Virginia

2020

Shooting Iron Horses:
Photographing Your Model Railroad

By J. Norman Reid and Jeffrey J. Fleisher

Published by Cobbler Mountain Press
3886 Ashville Road
Delaplane, Virginia 20144 USA

© Copyright 2020 J. Norman Reid and Jeffrey J. Fleisher All rights Reserved

All photographs © copyright 2020 J. Norman Reid and Jeffrey J. Fleisher

ISBN 978-1-71697-291-1

Preface

This book is about how to make good quality photographs and videos of model railroading. We were inspired to write it for several reasons.

- We observed that photos in club competitions were often poorly composed, badly exposed and generally below the quality merited by the models they displayed.
- We've seen newsletter editors struggle to get photos that reproduce effectively in the black & white format that's usually needed for inexpensive printing.
- While we see magazine editors calling for more submissions, many modelers are reluctant to respond because they don't know what's required or how to meet those requirements.
- Although videos are now nearly everywhere on the web, many are badly lit or don't show the models to best advantage.

We are unaware of any other book on photographing and videoing model railroads, so—given the explosion in interest in model railroad photography—we believed the time was right to fill the void.

We each have long-standing backgrounds in both model railroading and photography. Norm's serious interest in photography began when his father loaned him an Argus and continued when he was the photographer for his high school and college newspapers and yearbooks. He has published other books on photography, as well as articles and photos in model railroading and other magazines and books. He began model railroading with an American Flyer set he received at age 6. This developed into an S scale layout he operated until a move forced him to downsize to a small N scale layout. Another move created a hiatus until he and Jeff recently decided to build the North Fork & Crooked Run Railway in HO scale in a corner of Jeff's woodshop. Norm's interest in steam locomotives and 1940s and 1950s freight cars has been rekindled and he has collected brass models from several railroads, principally the Nickel Plate, along whose tracks he played as a boy.

Jeff built an HO layout with his sons when they were growing up, then put it away after they grew up and moved away. Now that his grandsons are of an age to be interested in trains, he decided to build a new layout and invited Norm to join in. Jeff's principal interest is in creating detailed structures and scenes using craftsman kits. Jeff has had a long interest in photography starting in high school and then formalized with a master's degree in Photographic Science and Instrumentation from the Rochester Institute of Technology. He worked for 34 years in research and development for the Central Intelligence Agency, dealing with satellite imagery collection and analysis. His interest continues today, focusing on macro and close-up photography and exploring the interesting effects of infrared photography. He and Norm are also authoring a book on macrophotography that explores many of the practices and skills needed for the best model railroad photography.

Norman Reid
Jeffrey Fleisher
May 2020

CONTENTS

Preface i

Contents iii

Acknowledgements v

Introduction vii

Chapter 1 Making a Quick Start 1

Shooting Scenes in Miniature 1
Photographing Deep Scenes 3
Extreme Close-Ups 3
Making Cover Shots 4
Creating Videos 4
Getting Started 5

Chapter 2 Shooting for Best Effect 7

Shoot Like It's a Real Railroad 7
Tell a Story 8
Choosing Good Angles and Positions 9
   Adjust Your Camera's Angle 9
   Positioning the Subject Within the Frame 10
   Horizons and Depth in Scenes 11
Use Leading Lines 12
Choose Unusual Viewpoints 13
Rotate Your Camera 13
Conduct Border Patrol 14
Include People and Details 14
Use Repetition 15
Keep Visual Balance 16
Use the Rule of Odds 16
Make Some Smoke 16
   Use Cotton 16
   Paint Smoke on Glass 16
   Add Smoke in Post-Processing 17
   Grab Some Real Smoke 18

Chapter 3 Making Still Photographs 19

Managing Exposure 19
Maximizing Depth of Field 20
   Understanding F-stops 20
   Enter the Zone of Confusion 21
How to Focus Stack 21
   Things to Consider 24
   Focus Stacking Methods 24
   Processing Stacks 24
Factors Affecting Image Quality 25
   Cut Camera Noise 25
   Minimize Vibrations 25
   Use Only Optical Zoom 25
Do Your Housekeeping 25
   Clean Your Lens 25
   Guard Your Sensor 25
   Eliminate Clutter 26
   Clean the Layout 26
   Use Your Lens Hood 26
   Make Test Shots 26
Using Backgrounds 26
   Permanent Backgrounds 26
   Temporary Backgrounds 26
   Natural Backgrounds 27

Chapter 4 Lighting Your Scenes 29

Choosing Among Types of Lighting 29
Setting the Quantity and Quality of Lighting 30
Position Your Lights for the Effect You Want 31
   Using Two-Light Setups 31
   Softening Shadows 32
Painting with Light 33
Special Lighting Situations 33
   Freezing Motion 33
   Showing the Time of Day 34
Lighting for Video 34

Chapter 5 Photos for Documentation 37

Making Photos for Sales 37
Photos for Insurance and Estate Documenta-

tion 37
    Insurance Documentation 37
    Estate Planning 38

Chapter 6 Shooting Trains in Motion 41
Shooting from a Static Position 41
Other Possibilities 41
The Mechanics of Making Videos 41
Using Video Equipment 42

Chapter 7 Backdrop Photographs 45
Shooting Panoramas 45
Printing Backdrops 45
    Individual Prints 45
    Continuous Rolls 46
Mounting Backdrops 46

Chapter 8 Post-Processing 47
Calibrate Your Monitor 47
Set Up Your Paper 47
Editing Software 48
Focus Stacking Photos 50
Special Post-Processing Issues 50
Processing Video 50

Chapter 9 Completing the Job 53
Posting Photos to the Web 53
Prints for Contests or Displays 53
Photos for Newsletters 54
Photos for Presentations 55
Photos for Publication 55
Videos for the Web 56

Chapter 10 Gearing Up 57
Choosing a Camera 57
    Smartphones 57
    Point and Shoot Cameras 57
    DSLRs 58
    Mirrorless Cameras 60
    Focus Stacking Capability 60
    Film Cameras 61
    Video Cameras 61
Lenses and Lens Modifiers 61
    Lenses 62
    Lens Modifiers 63
Tripods and Related Gear 65
    Stabilizing the Camera 65
    Aiding Composition 66
    Doing Other Things 66
    Desirable Features 66
    Bean Bags as an Alternative 66
    Gorillapods 67
    Smartphone Tripods 67
    Selfie Sticks 67
    Tripod Heads 68
Lighting Equipment 69
    Reflectors and Diffusers 69
    Portable Lights 69
    Flash 69
    LEDs 70
    Ring Lights 70
    Softboxes 71
Focusing Rails 71
    Stackshot 72
    Helicon Remoto 72
Focus Stacking Software 72

Conclusion 75

Acknowledgements

The authors thank the following persons, who provided access to their model railroad layouts for photography: Mark Gionet; Wolfgang Neudorfer; and Sandy Robeck, President of the Northern Virginia Model Railroaders.

They would also like to thank Tony Koester and Brett Wiley for their helpful comments on an earlier draft.

Ellen Fleisher did a masterful job of proofreading the final text and saved us from many errors.

Norm thanks his wife Betsy for her patience and support in this and all his many endeavors. Without her loving care, this book would neither have been possible nor worthwhile.

Jeff would like to thank his grandsons Anthony and Aiden for showing an interest in model railroading and rekindling his desire to build a new layout with their help. Jeff would also like to thank his wife, Ellen, for all her encouragement towards building the new layout and in the writing of this book and her loving patience in his woodworking, photography and model railroading hobbies.

Introduction

To borrow from the title of a 1969 Sydney Pollack film, "They shoot iron horses, don't they?" That's another way of saying that making photos and videos of our model railroads is popular, and now more than ever. The flood of inexpensive cameras and video gear has made model photography widely accessible. Now nearly everyone who wants to photograph their miniature trains can do so.

But why photograph your models in the first place? There are lots of reasons. For many model railroaders, it's the desire to show off their craftsmanship on Facebook, in blogs or elsewhere on the web. Club newsletters need photos from individual or club layouts. And some model railroad organizations such as the NMRA sponsor photo competitions at their annual gatherings, offering the chance to compete for prizes and recognition. Many modelers want to sell their surplus trains on eBay or other auction sites and need good quality photos to help buyers see what they are getting and bring higher prices. Modelers with major investments in their models and layouts need documentation for insurance and estate purposes. Finally, photographing your layout can help improve the composition of your scenes by revealing in photos what you may otherwise fail to see.

If these reasons weren't enough, many modelers make presentations at club meetings or conduct clinics at larger conferences. The quality of photos in on-screen projections can make or break a presentation and professional-level photography is a plus in these settings. This is even more true for photos intended for publication in magazines and books, where special requirements must be met and only the best will do.

The ability to post videos to Facebook or YouTube, combined with the miniaturization of video cameras, has led to an explosion in model railroad videos and opened an entirely new field for model railroad photography.

In addition to these reasons, this fact remains: making and showing photos of your layout is simply fun!

We have three major objectives in this book:

- To explain the steps needed to make outstanding photos of your trains and layouts
- To demystify the processes for making high quality photos and videos
- To help you avoid common mistakes and adopt best photo and video practices

In this book you'll learn:

- What makes effective subjects for model railroad photos and videos
- How lighting can make or break your photos
- How to make your best shots
- How to process your photos and videos once you've made them
- How you can use your photos and videos in a variety of ways
- What you'll need in the way of gear and how to choose it

The book's chapters cover everything you'll need to know about making good photos and videos and processing them for final use. Though the book can be read from start to finish, you may prefer to jump straight to those chapters that address topics of immediate interest. That's OK too. We've written each chapter so it can stand alone and so the book can be read in any sequence or only selectively. It's your book. Use it the way that works best for you. Because you may already have all the gear you'll need, we've postponed that topic to chapter 10. But if you're just starting out or are thinking of upgrading your gear, you may want to begin there.

So, all aboard! This train is now leaving the station for all points east and west, north and south. There'll be a few bumps along the way, with some curves and a few grades to climb, but we aim to make your journey as smooth and fun-filled as possible. And now, tickets please!

Chapter 1 Making a Quick Start

For many model railroaders, photographing their layouts represents something new and unfamiliar. Though we've built skills in laying track, building structures and constructing scenery, making good photos of our miniature empires may seem daunting. But it need not be so.

Though model railroad photography can involve new equipment and new skills, it's likely that you already have enough of both to get started. No doubt you have a digital camera or smartphone that you use for family or vacation pictures. If so, you've got what you need to get underway.

You'll find you can make quality photos easily with the gear you've got now and your current methods of photography. In this chapter, we'll show you how to put them to use making common types of shots. Then, in later chapters we'll go deeper to show how you can use even more advanced techniques to make specialized kinds of photos. So, let's get started.

Shooting Scenes in Miniature

Probably the most common type of photo you'll want to make is of a single small scene on your layout. Photo 1 is an example.

Your goal in photographing scenes like this is to include everything you want to show while leaving out elements that don't contribute to the message you want to convey. And, you'll want to show them in pleasing arrangements that have visual impact.

How you position your camera or smartphone will affect the look you'll get in your photos. Frequently, photos are taken from a 45° angle above the scene. See Figure 1. This provides the viewer with an overall sense of the scene and is probably the most common perspective shown in magazine photos.

But an effective alternative is to photograph at eye level to the rolling stock or the figures that populate the scene. This results in a more intimate view, the perspective a railfan would have on a day's outing. See Figure 2.

Photo 1. Many photos of model railroads will feature a small portion of a layout or diorama containing a single scene, such as this one on the Northern Virginia Model Railroaders layout in Vienna, Virginia.

Figure 1. Model railroad photos are frequently made from a 45-degree angle, which gives an overall perspective on a scene.

Figure 2. Eye level shots reflect a realistic view, the one a railfan would have from a standing position trackside.

Photo 2. Eye level shots approximate the perspective a railfan would have when chasing real trains and result in more intimate and realistic views. The photo was made on Mark Gionet's Boston and Maine Western Route layout.

The most important consideration in setting up mini scenes such as this is what we call border patrol. Make sure there are no offending intrusions at the fringes of the scene, such as stray tree branches or building corners that are just out of place. Make everything in the picture contribute to the scene. We discuss these and more ideas for creating effective scenes in detail in Chapter 2.

Photographing Deep Scenes

Some of the scenes you'll want to photograph may extend deep into your layout. Consider a rail line that disappears into the distance, or a long train of coal hoppers negotiating an S-curve at the base of a cliff. In these cases, you'll face a special challenge—getting as much of the scene as possible in sharp focus. For that, you'll need what's called a high depth of field (DOF).

The typical way to achieve a high DOF is to focus your camera one-third of the way into the scene and choose a high f-stop number such as f/22 on your lens. These techniques will give you maximum sharpness throughout the scene without using a special method called focus stacking. We discuss these techniques, including focus stacking, in detail in Chapter

Extreme Close-Ups

Sometimes you may have small detail you want to emphasize, such as the close-up of an engine front or part of a mini scene. Your objective in this case is to have the principal subject in sharp focus but possibly separated from the background by letting it fall into unsharpness.

This type of photo is what photographers refer to as close-up or, if the focus is tight enough, macrophotography. The closer the focus, and the larger the subject is reproduced, the more special lenses may be called for. Macro lenses are special lenses that let you get in extremely close and magnify the size of your trains or characters. We discuss macro lenses and related gear in Chapter 10.

Photo 3. This image, from the Northern Virginia Model Railroaders layout, shows a typical scene of hand laid track disappearing into a distant tunnel. Although this image was made using the highest depth of field possible from a single photo, as we discuss in Chapter 3, there is a way to improve the sharpness of the track in the distance by using a technique called focus stacking.

Photo 4. Extreme close-ups emphasize tiny details in your models. Focusing close, as in the case of this Nickel Plate USRA 0-8-0 switcher, puts some of the details in sharp focus, while blurring the background and surrounding details.

Photo 5. This photo is a candidate for a book cover because it was shot in portrait mode and leaves room at the top for the book's title. The photo was made on Wolfgang Neudorfer's layout set in Germany.

Making Cover Shots

You may want to shoot a photo that can be used for a newsletter or maybe even a magazine. Cover photos are usually shot vertically so they are in portrait mode. Often, they're shot at a higher angle such as 45° so they convey more depth in the scene. And, they are arranged so the principal content is in the bottom two-thirds of the frame, leaving uncluttered room for the title or magazine masthead at the top.

Cover photos have special technical requirements for quality, especially when they're intended for the major magazines. We discuss this issue in more detail in Chapter 9.

Creating Videos

Digital technology has brought making videos within the grasp of model railroaders everywhere. Using your smartphone or most digital cameras, you can create interesting sequences of your trains running through your miniature landscape. You can even edit a series of sequences into a longer program.

The key to good videos is to support your camera so you don't end up with a lot of disturbing jerking in the final product. We provide some hints for making good videos in Chapter 6 and suggest a way to edit your videos and post them to Facebook or YouTube in Chapter 9.

Getting Started

These tips will get you quickly underway making photos of your layout. But, as in all things, there is even more you can do to make your photos and videos the best they can be. Especially if publication is your goal, you'll want to delve further. We'll help you do that in the chapters that follow.

Chapter 2 Shooting for Best Effect

If you're going to take the trouble to photograph your layout, you want to be sure your photos are the best they can be. In this chapter we'll outline some things you can do to assure they don't come out ho-hum.

Shoot Like It's a Real Railroad

To make your model railroad photos realistic, you'll want to shoot from the same angles you would a real railroad. Usually, this means shooting from ground level. To achieve this effect, you'll want to position your camera so it is at or near eye level to the layout scene.

But other positions are possible. Some real railroad photos are shot from bridges or overpasses, the tops of buildings and even trees. So, don't neglect these angles as alternative viewpoints. However, it's important to keep the angles realistic and not shoot from angles you could not duplicate in real life.

Photo 6. This image of a steam locomotive was taken from just above ground level and gives an almost eye-level perspective on the scene. The pictured model is on Wolfgang Neudorfer's layout set in Onhes-org, Germany.

Photo 7. This shot from above the track level simulates a photo taken from a bridge or signal tower. This photo was composed from a stack of 15 images combined using Helicon Focus.

Tell a Story

In composing your scene, consider what the elements are saying as you're presenting them. Do they have a story to tell? What is happening in the scene? What has just occurred or is about to occur? The best scenes have a tale to share with viewers. Arrange your composition so the elements you're showing present a clear message. The message does not need to be complex. But it does need to appeal to viewers so they become engaged in the scene.

At the same time, remove any elements from the scene that do not contribute to the story. This will sharpen your message by eliminating misleading or distracting features.

Photo 8. There's a clear story in this scene of an oarsman struggling to row his boat away from the dock in rough water. The scene is on Mark Gionet's Boston & Maine Western Route layout. All the elements in the scene contribute to its overall success.

Choosing Good Angles and Positions

The most important thing you can do is to clarify the main point of interest in your photo, both in still photos and videos. Do this by moving in or zooming in close to cut out extraneous details. Too many elements in your photo will confuse your viewers. You'll find that simplicity in your photo composition is often the most effective technique.

> Simplicity in your photo composition is often the most effective technique.

Adjust Your Camera's Angle

The angle at which you shoot your layout, especially your trains, will have a big impact on the impression you make. Shooting from a low angle will tend to exaggerate the impact of the scene, while shooting from a high angle diminishes it. Also, when you set up your scenes, experiment by moving the camera from one side to another. Sometimes even slight movements to the left or right can dramatically affect your composition.

Photo 9. The trolley and bus at the Salisbury, NC, station on the Northern Virginia Model Railroaders layout were shot from a high angle and the photo shows the overall scheme of the scene. Shooting from a higher angle simulates a railfan shot from the top of a nearby tower or building.

Photo 10. Here are the same trolley and bus photographed from near ground level. Low-level shots offer a more intimate viewing experience.

Photo 11. The locomotives leading the passenger train are posed at the right side of the image, leading the train out of the frame. This image can be improved by repositioning the camera.

Positioning the Subject Within the Frame

How you place the subject of primary interest within the camera's frame also matters. Avoid placing it in the dead center to keep your photos move lively. If your subject is being shown in motion, such as a locomotive, allow some leading space ahead of it so it has some place to move into.

A classic practice of landscape photographers is to follow the Rule of Thirds. If you divide the camera's frame into thirds with horizontal and vertical lines, you'll create a 3 x 3 grid. You'll often achieve the greatest visual impact by positioning the subject at one intersection of the grid lines.

Photo 12. This image of the same scene has the locomotives positioned leading into the scene, giving them visual space to move into the frame. For this reason, it's a much stronger image. Both photos were made on Mark Gionet's Boston & Maine Western Route layout.

Photo 13. The nose of the locomotive is approaching the one-third point in the frame, a classic technique to set the point of focus for attracting attention. However, like all "rules" of composition, this one should not be slavishly followed and there are times when the Rule of Thirds can and should be creatively broken. The photo was made on the Northern Virginia Model Railroader's layout.

Horizons and Depth in Scenes

Another issue is where to place the horizon in your photo. It's best to avoid putting it in the dead center, since that tends to create dull photos. Instead, when you put the horizon low in the frame you can create an impression of intimacy in the scene.

On the other hand, when you put the horizon high in the frame you can include more foreground details, building a sense of depth to the scene. Landscape photographers know to include elements in the foreground, middle ground and background to emphasize depth, and you should do so as well. Another way to create depth is to place larger elements in the foreground and smaller ones in the background. Overlapping the background with foreground elements such as trees, bushes,

Photo 14. This scene from Wolfgang Neudorfer's layout was shot from a low angle, permitting the background to be visible and emphasizing greater intimacy in the scene.

buildings and even people is yet another technique for simulating distance.

Photo 15. Another scene on Wolf Neudorfer's layout, this one shot with the implied horizon high in the frame, which emphasizes the train in the foreground against the beautiful painted backdrop.

Photo 16. This photo of Wolfgang Neudorfer's layout includes sharply focused details from the foreground, middle ground and background and displays maximum depth. It was created with a stack of 21 individual images combined using Helicon Focus. Focus stacking is discussed in Chapter 3.

Photo 17. At times, it may be desirable to place the emphasis on foreground elements, such as this Series G-10 (Munich) boxcar with brakeman's cab, by using a lower f-stop to allow the background to go out of focus. The model, part of Wolfgang Neudorfer's layout, dates from the 1920s-1930s.

Use Leading Lines

Landscape photographers know to use leading lines to draw viewers' interest. Your photos and videos will be enhanced when you use lines to point to the subject of principal interest. Straight lines that recede into the distance, such as railroad tracks, show perspective. Lines that cross the frame diagonally are the most energetic and convey a sense of action. Horizontal lines, by contrast, are static and passive. Curved lines, especially those forming an S-curve, are a graceful way to contribute interest in any scene.

Photo 18. The curved lines of the hand laid track lead the eye through the scene and into the distance at right, creating a pleasant perspective. The image is balanced left and right by the trackage and platform on the right and Salisbury station on the left. The scene is a part of the extensive layout of the Northern Virginia Model Railroaders in Vienna, Virginia.

Photo 19. The hopper at the Spencer engine facility forms a slight diagonal line, creating more visual interest by suggesting greater movement and dynamism than if it were completely horizontal. The scene is from the Northern Virginia Model Railroaders Vienna, Virginia, layout.

Photo 20. Here the track leads the eye into the depths of this scene on Mark Gionet's Boston & Maine Western Route layout.

Choose Unusual Viewpoints

When possible, choose unusual viewpoints. Rather than shooting everything at eye level, that is, from a trackside view, shoot from

Photo 21. This antiques store on Mark Gionet's Boston & Maine Western Route layout appears to be taken from the top of a nearby roof, a realistic potential shooting location for a railfan.

under trees, from rooftop level or the tops of rolling stock. The helicopter view, while sometimes useful to show the design of a layout, is easily overdone.

Rotate Your Camera

The orientation of your camera matters also. Because cameras are arraanged horizontally, shooting everything in landscape mode is an easy trap to fall into. But some scenes are best composed vertically. Don't neglect this angle, especially if you're planning to shoot a magazine cover. The orientation of video cameras, on the other hand, is governed by the horizontal screens for which they're shooting and they'll normally be positioned in landscape format.

Photo 22. Include vertically-oriented photos where it fits your subject, such as this turntable on Wolfgang Neudorfer's layout. If you are shooting for a magazine cover, be sure to allow space at the top of the frame for the magazine's masthead.

Conduct Border Patrol

Be sure to inspect the edges of your frame carefully before you release the shutter. Extraneous elements like the unwanted corner of a building or an out-of-place tree can ruin a model railroad photo as surely as the old telephone pole growing out of a head ruins the portrait of a person.

Photo 23. This photo of an interesting scene in Salisbury, NC, would be stronger if the light pole on the left was eliminated. Simply cropping the photo more tightly would do the job. It's important to inspect the view in your camera before shooting to minimize the need for adjustments after the fact. The Salisbury terminal building is from the Northern Virginia Model Railroaders layout.

Include People and Details

As we've already indicated, you'll often want to choose a single main element as your focus. Nonetheless, to create interest in your scenes, the principal element needs to be supported by details, preferably lots of them. Both people and objects populate the most effective scenes. It's important that when you include people they be doing something that contributes to the overall action in the scene.

Photo 24.. The activities of the passengers preparing to board the coach are the primary point of interest in this photo made on Wolfgang Neudorfer's layout.

14

Use Repetition

Repetition of objects is a trick used by landscape photographers to create drama and interest. You can follow their lead by incorporating series of such things as railroad ties, telephone poles, fence posts, chimneys, and rooftop angles that repeat.

Photo 25. This chain link fence is an example of a repeated element. Repetitions can be effective components of photos and are often used by professional photographers for their strong graphic qualities. This photo was made on Mark Gionet's Alexandria, Virginia, Boston & Maine Western Route layout.

Keep Visual Balance

Another concept to bear in mind is the issue of visual balance within the frame. Subjects that dominate one side of the frame may appear unbalanced if there isn't something on the other side to offer visual weight. When each side is in relative balance, the resulting symmetrical appearance seems harmonious. Unbalanced scenes, by contrast, are asymmetrical; they imply action, dynamism and disharmony. Neither of these is right or wrong. They simply express differing impressions to which you'll want to be alert.

Photo 27. Here is an example of the Rule of Odds in which two sets of three figures are positioned in the scene, the workers entering the manhole and the spectators on the sidewalk. Groups of three objects have balance and are visually satisfying. The scene is on the Northern Virginia Model Railroaders layout in Vienna, Virginia.

Photo 26. The visual weight in this image is clearly on the left side, where the tonnage of the caboose rests. The workers on the right provide balance to the image, which would be lacking if they were not present. The scene is of a yard between Salisbury and Spencer, NC, on the Northern Virginia Model Railroaders layout.

Use the Rule of Odds

A final principle is the "Rule of Odds." Many photographers believe an odd number of main elements is more visually pleasing than an even number. Three often seems to be a good number of main elements to include in any scene. Though you may have many more minor details, too many principal objects can easily make a scene overcrowded and confusing.

Make Some Smoke

For still photos, especially those including steam locomotives, you may want to show smoke and steam in your images. There are several ways to do this.

Use Cotton

The most time-honored method is to use cotton battens or shredded cotton balls to simulate smoke and steam. To use this technique, shred cotton to simulate steam emanating from the valves or smoke from the smokestack. Smoke is more realistic if it's at least somewhat black, so you may want to darken it with a little black paint or dye sprayed on the cotton. To keep the smoke from appearing toylike, make your photo using a time exposure so you can move the cotton to blur its outline. You can do this by attaching a bit of transparent thread to the end of the cotton and moving it during the time exposure. Another method is to use a hair dryer or small fan to gently blow the cotton while the camera's shutter is open.

Paint Smoke on Glass

A more effective method is to paint simulated smoke and steam on a sheet of glass or a clear plastic photographic filter and shoot your images through the glass. With this method, it's a lot easier to achieve the density and color of smoke and steam you are looking for. Diesel locomotives, whose exhaust is typically more subtle, can easily be photographed by this method. The primary difficulty lies in the fact that you may need to paint the effect on the glass while looking through the viewfinder to get the smoke in the right position.

Add Smoke in Post-Processing

The best results will be obtained by making your photos without smoke, then adding it during post-processing using Adobe Photoshop or another editing program. This gives you the most control and artistic license, but it comes at the price of purchasing and learning to use the software. An advantage, though, lies in being able to simultaneously represent valve steam and feathers while also modeling darker clouds of smoke. This is achieved by painting the smoke and steam effects on a duplicate layer that overlaps the basic image. In this section we'll describe our method for doing it.

There are many videos online showing how to make a brush in Photoshop by starting with a picture of a cloud. The goal is to produce a brush with a very random outline shape. Rather than starting with a picture of a cloud, you can download many free versions of smoke brushes that will give the same results as if you had created your own using a cloud picture.

However, having a brush with a very random outline is only the starting point. If you use the brush without modifying any of the brush parameters, you'll end up with a very uniform color and no texture or variation of detail. Photo 28 shows a smoke brush with no modification.

For realistic results, you'll need to modify the brush settings. Although a variety of categories of settings exist, we've had success playing with the brush Shape Dynamics, Scattering, Color Dynamics, and Opacity. The settings can be changed in Photoshop's Brush Settings dialog. See Figure 3.

Photo 28. In this image, the smoke effects were created without varying the brush details. The result is clearly unacceptable.

To produce the following picture, we used these settings:

Shape Dynamics:

Size Jitter: 100%

Angle Jitter 20-50%

These settings randomly change the size and angle of the brush while dragging it.

Scattering:

Scatter: 40%

This setting randomly changes the pattern as you drag the brush.

Color Dynamics:

Foreground/Background jitter: 15%

This setting randomly adjusts the amount of foreground/background color.

Figure 3. The Photoshop screen for adding smoke using the brushes.

Opacity:

Opacity setting: various

Opacity controls the density of the smoke. You can darken the smoke by increasing the opacity or making multiple passes with the brush over the same area.

By adjusting these settings, you can produce an image with simulated smoke as shown in Photo 29.

To accomplish this, you import both your model railroad photograph and your image of a locomotive with live smoke into the post-processing program as separate layers. Then, using the editing tools of the software and working on the image of the life-size locomotive, mask off the locomotive and surroundings, leaving only the smoke you wish to copy. Next, copy the smoke image from that layer and paste it onto the layer of the model railroad photo with the smoke positioned where you want it to rest.

Photo 29. The smoke and steam issuing from this locomotive were added in Photoshop by painting on a duplicate layer of the basic image, with adjustments to the opacity of the steam. The original photo was made on the layout of the Northern Virginia Model Railroaders Club.

Grab Some Real Smoke

Yet another option is to cut and paste images of smoke from real locomotives into your model railroad photos. This is another application for Photoshop or another editing program.

The challenges with this technique are to find real examples of locomotive smoke that are configured in the same orientation and location as your model railroad engine and to position the copied smoke so it appears real.

Chapter 3 Making Still Photographs

Much, and perhaps all, of your photography will be of static objects, that is, trains and structural details that are frozen in motion. You can do several things to ensure you've made the best, sharpest photos. A lot of it has to do with getting as much of your scenes as possible in sharp focus. But to achieve realistic-looking photos, you'll also need to plan your backgrounds carefully. We take up these topics in this chapter.

First, to improve your photography in general, and for model railroad photography in particular, there are some good practices you should incorporate into your techniques. Always be thinking about the effects of lighting, vibrations, image quality and depth-of-field on your final picture. In addition, be sure you understand the relationship among the shutter speed, aperture size and ISO (camera speed) settings to get the highest quality picture with the emotional impact you are trying to achieve.

We'll briefly discuss each of these topics. While some of this discussion may seem a little technical, and it is, it's important to understand how your camera works and why a picture looks the way it does. Let's start with the exposure triangle.

Managing Exposure

There's a direct relationship among the camera's shutter speed, aperture setting and ISO speed, and how these are set will influence how your picture will look. If you use a slow shutter speed and a train is moving through your scene, it may be blurred; but if you use a fast shutter speed, the train will be sharp. If you use a wide-open aperture setting, the object you focused on will be sharp, but objects in front of and behind it may be out of focus. If you use a very small aperture opening, the whole picture may be in focus. Finally, by adjusting the ISO speed from a small number to high number, you can shoot in lower light levels or with a faster shutter speed, though at the expense of more digital noise in your picture.

What is the exposure triangle? It's the relationship among these three functions. To get a correctly exposed picture you need to balance the relationship among these three parameters. This means that if you slow down the camera's shutter speed, you need to make the aperture smaller to let in less light. If you speed up the shutter speed you need to make the aperture larger to get the same amount of light onto the camera's sensor. And, if you want to maintain a higher shutter speed or smaller aperture in low light levels, you'll need to increase the ISO to make the camera's sensor more sensitive.

> The exposure triangle is the relationship between shutter speed, aperture opening, and ISO, or digital speed. Because they are mutually dependent, if you change any one of them, the others are affected and must be adjusted to compensate.

All digital cameras work this way. You may not realize that your smartphone camera is making these adjustments for you automatically, but it is, as does your point and shoot camera. More sophisticated cameras like DSLRs give you more control over these parameters. In fact, when you select different camera modes on your smartphone or point and shoot camera—the flower for closeups or the runner for fast action—the camera is adjusting these parameters for you automatically behind the scenes.

The moral is that you can affect how your picture looks by taking control of these settings. If you want to show motion in your picture by having the train slightly blurred, use a slower shutter speed. If the train is speeding through your scene or you want to make your photos without a tripod, use a faster shutter speed. You have this type of control with any adjustable camera you may be using.

Maximizing Depth of Field

Depth of field is the region in front of and behind the subject that appears to your eye to be in focus. In reality, only the object that you actually focus on is truly in focus, and the area in front and in back goes gradually out of focus until it becomes noticeable to your eye. This apparently in-focus area, called the circle of confusion, gets larger as the camera's aperture gets smaller (higher f-stop number). Using the smallest possible aperture opening will yield the largest in-focus area within your photo.

Depth of field is important to consider when setting up to photograph a scene on your layout. You need to understand which parts of the scene will be in focus and which may be out of focus. Obviously, the main element of your scene, whether a locomotive, a highly detailed structure or a landscape element like a tunnel portal, is typically set to be in sharp focus. Depending on your camera's aperture setting, some portion in front of the main element and some portion behind the main element will be out of focus. Depth of field can be controlled to some extent by regulating the size of your camera's aperture. In single images, it can also be helped by where you position the point of focus. But where these techniques do not suffice, a technique called focus stacking can produce a scene that is completely in focus, from front to back.

> Depth of field is the portion of your scene that appears to be in sharp focus. It can be regulated to some extent by adjusting the size of your lens's aperture.

Focus stacking is a new technique that allows you to have almost unlimited depth-of-field. You can increase the effective depth-of-field by taking multiple images at different focus points and then combining them in post-processing. This technique is described fully later in this chapter. You need to experiment with it to understand how it works and whether it will give you a pleasing picture. In the real world, our eyes focus on only one area and other areas are out of focus, so looking at a scene that is 100 percent in focus may be unnatural. It may be very useful when taking a closeup of a locomotive or rolling stock, if you want it to be completely in focus. But, it may be less useful when taking a picture of a portion of your layout. That is up to you to decide.

It's commonly believed that longer lenses such as telephoto lenses have shallower depth of field than lenses with shorter focal lengths. In one sense that's true; in another it's not. With the camera in a fixed position, say, on a tripod, you'll find that a shorter focal length lens will yield more depth of field than a longer lens will from the same camera position. But if you move the camera's position so longer and shorter focal length lenses produce the same size image, you'll discover that your lenses will have identical depths of field. You can, therefore, achieve the same depth of field with any lens by moving closer to or away from your subject, depending on the lens you are using.

Understanding F-stops

A camera's aperture size controls both the amount of light entering the camera and the range of area that's in focus around your main subject. On DSLR and mirrorless cameras this is controlled by adjusting the camera's f-stops. The smaller the f-stop number (e.g., f/2.8), the larger the aperture opening and the shallower the depth of field. The larger the f-stop number (e.g., f/22), the smaller the aperture opening and the greater the depth of field. Confusing, right?

On point-and-shoot cameras, you can control the depth of field by selecting one of the scene description icons. For example, a flower icon usually means a slow shutter speed and small aperture setting, while a runner icon may give you a fast shutter speed and wide aperture. You can experiment with these settings to see what works for your setup.

Photo 30. A brass Nickel Plate Mikado shot at f/3.0 with the focus on the builder's plate.

Photo 31. The same locomotive photographed at f/8.0 at the same focus point. The higher f-stop brings more of the model into focus, but large parts are still unsharp.

Photo 32. At f/22, even more of the locomotive is in focus, and the tender is now beginning to appear sharp.

Photo 33. At f/36, most of the locomotive and tender are now in focus, though the rear of the tender is still a little unsharp.

While using small apertures helps greatly to increase depth of field, it's not always enough, as Photos 30 to 33 show. Even at a very small f-stop such as f/36 you may not be able to get your whole subject in focus.

Enter the Zone of Confusion

A technique familiar from film camera days is to use what's known as the zone of confusion. In effect, depth of field is found to be greatest when the focus point is placed about a third of the way into the scene. The zone of confusion is the area both in front of and behind the focus point that appears to be in sharp focus. Focusing a third of the way into a scene, combined with a small f-stop, will produce the sharpest possible image over the widest range of depth within your scene.

> Focusing a third of the way into a scene, combined with a small f-stop, will produce the sharpest possible image over the widest range of depth within your scene.

How to Focus Stack

However, using high f-stops and focusing a third of the way into the scene still doesn't always suffice to get completely sharp images. Digital technology has made possible a new technique, focus stacking, that can extend depth of field even further. To focus stack, you create a series of images, each at a slightly different focus point, then combine them into a single image in post-processing. Several post-processing software packages are available for this purpose.

Focus stacking was originally developed for closeup and macro photography, and it can be readily applied to scenes on your layout. In photographing your layout, you can make separate images of the foreground, middle ground and background and then combine them into a single in-focus image.

To understand how focus stacking works, you need to understand the relationship between the lens aperture size and depth of field. As we've said, when you focus the camera on a subject, only one point in the image is in sharpest focus. As you move away from that point, either in front or behind, the point slowly goes out of focus. The range that your eye perceives as being in focus is called the depth of field.

At a small f-stop number (e.g., f/2.8) the aperture is large, which produces a very narrow depth of field.

As you increase to a larger f-stop number (e.g., f/22), the aperture diameter gets smaller and the depth of field increases.

When an even wider depth of field is required, you can use focus stacking to take multiple images, each at a different focus point, and then combine them into a single image in post-processing. Focus stacking is a sampling of multiple slices of in-focus positions within the scene. The first image is made with the closest point to the camera in focus. Then the focusing point is moved slightly and a second image is made. This is repeated, with a small change in focus between each shot, until the entire subject has been covered. While none of the individual images has the entire subject in focus, each image has a part of the subject in focus, so that when combined into a single image they show the entire subject in focus.

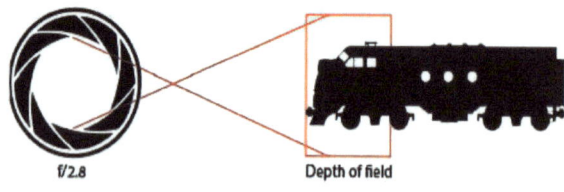

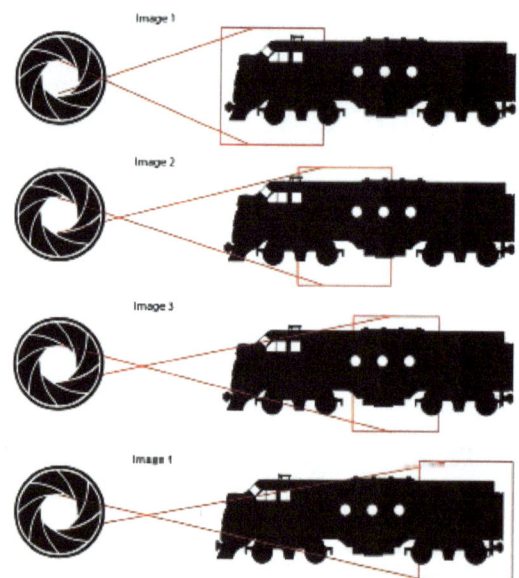

Figure 4. At a large diaphragm opening (small f-stop number), the image will have a small depth of field, so only a small portion of the image will be in sharp focus.

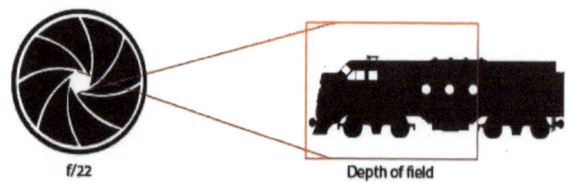

Figure 6. A sequence of photos with varying focal points that overlap can be combined into a stack that will produce a photo that is in sharp focus from front to back of the scene. Ordinarily, an f-stop such as f/8 or f/11 will be chosen to create a stack of photos, which will likely require many more than four images.

Figure 5. A smaller diaphragm opening (larger f-stop number) will produce a larger depth of field, so that more of the scene appears in sharp focus. However, even this may leave a part of the scene out-of-focus and blurry.

Photos 34 to 37 illustrate how focus stacking can produce a completely in-focus image. Each image shows an area in focus and then out-of-focus areas close to and far from the camera. Stacking these individual photos provides a completely in-focus image, as shown in Photo 38.

Photo 34. The first image has the hopper in focus.

Photo 35. The next photo moves the focus deeper into the scene so the rocks become sharper.

Photo 36. The third image brings the rocks into even sharper focus.

Photo 37. In the fourth image, the trees in the distance become sharper, but the foreground is out-of-focus.

Photo 38. The stacked photo resulting from the sequence of four individual photos shows the hopper, tipple and background trees in sharp focus. Had we also included photos of the weeds in the foreground in the stack, they too would have been rendered in focus. The depth of field in a stacked photo depends on the range of the scene included in the photo stack.

Things to Consider

There are several things to consider when creating a focus stack.

- As you turn the focus ring on your lens, you will notice a slight magnification shift of the image. Be sure to compose your subject with enough room around it to accommodate this magnification change. Focus on the front of the subject and then twist the focus ring to the furthest point in the image to make sure nothing that is important to the composition has moved out of the frame. If it has, readjust your composition and repeat this step until everything of importance remains in the frame at all focal points.
- Set the camera on manual exposure and adjust your exposure setting. You do not want the exposure to vary as you step through your stack.
- There is no optimal f-stop to use for focus stacking. The sharpest portion of a lens is normally at f/8 to f/11, but you may want to explore using your lens's widest aperture to have the focus fall off faster in order to intentionally blur the background. Remember, it's critical that the depth of field for each image overlaps the depth of field of the preceding image until you have reached the last image of your subject; then the focus can fall off to blur the background if you choose.
- We like to take an extra frame or two at the beginning and end of a stack to ensure that we have captured the total focus range desired. You can always discard any unneeded images during post-processing.

Focus Stacking Methods

One method of creating photo stacks is by making slight adjustments to the lens focusing ring between exposures. You can do this manually. But there are also software applications that can drive the focusing ring on your autofocus lens if it is so equipped. One such program, Helicon Remote, will help set the near and far focusing points and automatically compute the step increase needed for a given f-stop. When started, Helicon Remote will then step to each focus location and take exposures automatically.

You can also move the camera and lens instead. To do this you'll need to use a focusing rail, either a manual one with a micrometer screw adjustment or a motorized computer-driven one like the Stackshot. Focusing rails and the Stackshot are discussed in Chapter 10.

In addition, some camera models now incorporate focus stacking in their processing capability. These are discussed in Chapter 10.

Processing Stacks

Once you have collected your focus stack of images, the real meat of the process is the rendering software you use in post-processing the stack. Several software packages are available, but the most popular three are Adobe Photoshop, Helicon Focus and Zerene Stacker. Both Helicon Focus and Zerene Stacker offer free trial versions so you explore them prior to making a purchase.

Adobe Photoshop – Photoshop versions CS6 and beyond all have the ability to stack images. Photoshop first creates a separate layer from each image. You then use the Auto-align Layers and Auto-blend Layer functions to render the stacked image. Once the final image is created you can crop and process it as normal.

Helicon Focus—Helicon Focus is a powerful stand alone program that provides multiple algorithms for stack creation and editing tools to remove artifacts from the composited image. You can load images directly into Helicon Focus or you can link catalog programs like Adobe Lightroom and export images from there to Helicon Focus.

On1 Photo Raw—Focus stacking is a relatively new feature in this software package, with additional features promised in future releases. It offers fewer rendering methods than other packages, but is easy to use.

Zerene Stacker—Zerene Stacker, like Helicon Focus, provides multiple algorithms to process stacked images. Like Helicon Focus, Zerene Stacker provides editing tools to deal with artifacts and improve the results of one method or the other.

Factors Affecting Image Quality

A number of other things can affect your image quality; we'll touch on a few of them here.

Cut Camera Noise

The camera's ISO setting is similar to film speed in the old days. The faster the film speed, the more grain (noise) would show up in the final picture. The same is true of digital cameras. The higher the ISO, the more digital noise is introduced because you are asking the camera sensor to turn up the gain (sensitivity) at the expense of adding digital noise to the picture. Therefore, for the highest quality, use the lowest possible ISO setting to capture the picture you want.

Minimize Vibrations

The effects of camera vibration increase as the magnification of the subject increases. Since we will typically be taking closeups of locomotives, rolling stock and portions of a layout, we need to do everything possible to reduce camera vibrations. The easiest thing to do, and the best first step, is to use a tripod. This will eliminate camera shake from hand-holding the camera. DSLRs, mirrorless cameras, and most point and shoot cameras have built in threads for tripod mounts. You can get tripod holders for your smartphones as well. We discuss tripods and related gear in Chapter 10.

Next, use either the camera's self-timer, a mechanical cable release or an infrared (IR) remote control release to trip the shutter. This will eliminate the vibrations that result from manually pressing the shutter release with your finger.

Use Only Optical Zoom

Use optical zoom only; do not use digital zoom. DSLRs and mirrorless cameras use 100 percent optical zooms by using interchangeable lenses on the camera. Most point and shoot cameras, however, have a combination of optical zoom (physically moving the camera's lens position) and digital zoom (replicating pixels in software to simulate a closer image). Digital zoom adds noise to the image. Smartphone cameras use only digital zoom, but most have a very small zoom range, so the amount of noise may not be noticeable in the final image.

Do Your Housekeeping

Some caretaking practices should become second nature as you take pictures. Some of these follow.

Clean Your Lens

Continually clean your lens to remove dust particles, which may show up in your image. While many of these can be removed in post-processing, it's better to be conscientious up front to reduce your workload later.

Guard Your Sensor

Dust that settles on your camera's sensor is even more problematic. It will show up as dark specks on your images that must then be cloned out to get rid of them. You'll save much time in post-processing by keeping your camera's sensor clean. Avoid changing lenses in dusty or windy conditions and change them with the mirror pointed downward to discourage dust from settling on it. If you should end up with dust anyway, you can get a kit to clean the sensor yourself or send your camera out for professional cleaning.

Eliminate Clutter

Have a primary subject in your image and remove anything that doesn't support that subject. Scan the boundary of your viewfinder for objects sticking into the scene that detract from the main subject. For example, a layout with a bush or tree half cut-off at the edge of the picture may be distracting. Double check your viewfinder carefully before shooting to be sure things are properly composed and clear of intruding or distracting objects.

Clean the Layout

Dust and cobwebs will quickly ruin a shot. They seem to be inevitable and will often show up clearly in the close-up photos model railroad photography requires. A soft brush and a can of compressed air are good to have alongside to clean up details before you shoot.

Use Your Lens Hood

Use a lens hood to eliminate flare or light streaks, especially when shooting dioramas outside. Stray light across the front of your lens will reduce the overall contrast of the image and may even create light noise that renders the image useless.

Make Test Shots

The best way to assure you're making photos with good depth of field, proper lighting, and free from other errors is to make test shots, then view the results on the camera's LCD screen. After all, pixels are free, so it costs you nothing and may save you considerable time and exasperation.

USING BACKGROUNDS

Another factor to consider when setting up a photograph is the background of the scene. When shooting a full-size landscape, you typically have the sky or some natural landscape in the background of your scene. On your layout you might have a nicely painted background or panoramic image. However, you might also have a concrete wall that shows up in the corner of your scene, something you'll want to avoid! And, if you are taking a picture of a piece of rolling stock or individual structure, you may need to artificially introduce a background as well. Let's look at some options.

Permanent Backgrounds

If you are photographing a scene on your layout, you most likely have a background available to you. The important thing is to make sure you select a camera angle that fills the frame with the background. You don't want to see the top edge of the background in your picture.

Temporary Backgrounds

There are a couple of situations where you may need a temporary, movable background. If your camera angle is such that you can't get your permanent background into the scene, you can insert a temporary background behind your subject. For example, you could

Photo 39. A panorama is a good way to emphasize the impressive painted backdrop of Wolfgang Neudorfer's layout. This photo is composed of several images stitched together horizontally.

paint a neutral sky scene on a piece of matte or foam core board and place it behind your scene. A few temporary landscape items like bushes or grass will help hide the bottom seam between the background board and the foreground.

If you are photographing a single item like a piece of rolling stock or structure independent of the layout, you can create a seamless background using softboxes, lighting cubes or seamless paper or cloth backgrounds. This equipment is discussed in Chapter 10. The key factor is that it need not be expensive if you are creative. We've even placed items on a carpeted staircase to get a seamless background look.

Natural Backgrounds

Often, successful diorama photos can be made out-of-doors using an appropriate natural background. The objective in this instance is to find a location that matches well with the foreground represented by the diorama. You'll want a location free of telephone and electric wires and other intrusions that don't contribute to your planned scene. Typical scenes are forests, mountains, or fields, though urban settings may also work well. Which of these you choose will, of course, be governed by the nature of your diorama.

As with a temporary background, you'll want to position your diorama so the natural setting meets it in a way that enhances, not detracts, from the foreground, which is your principal interest. You'll probably want to keep it low in relation to the diorama so the natural foreground does not compete with your modeled foreground. But this is a case for trial and error, and you'll want to experiment with different elevations of the model in relation to the natural setting.

Photo 40. The background behind this diorama is a photographic panorama print made in Ten Sleep Canyon, Wyoming. Because it's moveable, it works well as a temporary background that allows multiple photographic angles.

Chapter 4 Lighting Your Scenes

When photographing your layout, your goal is to create the illusion of realism. To achieve this, you'll need not only to provide enough light to make your exposures, but you'll also want to reduce shadows that obscure details or are otherwise distracting or unrealistic.

Choosing Among Types of Lighting

First, you'll want to turn off your camera's flash. While it might provide plenty of light, that light, coming straight from the camera, will produce both flat lighting and harsh shadows. Neither is desirable. Instead, use ambient lighting or bounce the flash off a white ceiling to create soft overhead lighting. You can also use a diffusion dome over your flash.

> While your camera's flash may provide plenty of lighting, that light will be flat and create harsh shadows. Neither is desirable.

Quite acceptable photos can be made with ordinary overhead room light, without special lighting equipment. As we discuss below, the chief issue will be with the color temperature of the lighting, which is determined by whether it is ordinary incandescent lighting, fluorescent, or LED. If you are shooting your images in RAW format, you can correct for these variations when you process your images. If shooting in jpeg format, however, you will need to be aware of the lighting source's color temperature and account for it in your settings.

The best alternative is to use multiple lights from two or more angles. An important principle of lighting is that the larger the light source, the softer and less harsh the resulting effect. For this reason, softboxes are a good choice. They are available at reasonable prices in a variety of sizes. The larger sizes give the softest and best directional lighting, but for small scenes you don't need to go overboard. A softbox of 24 x 24 inches is a good size.

Softboxes are available for both flash and continuous lighting. The latter are less expensive, since they require only bulbs and avoid the need to also purchase flash units. Both fluorescent and LED versions are available. These have the advantage of being cool in operation, as compared with the photoflood bulbs used in earlier days. Continuous lighting also has the advantage of letting you see the effect of lighting placement on shadows, something you can only achieve with flash units through trial and error.

> An important principle of lighting is that the larger the light source, the softer and less harsh the resulting effect.

Another way to achieve a large light source is to bounce the light off the ceiling, if you have one that's white, or a large piece of poster board. The effect is like that of a lightbox in that it spreads the light broadly. It's an inexpensive way to light your layout that gives up nothing in the quality of lighting.

For small dioramas or individual pieces of rolling stock, lighting cubes may suffice as well. These cubes are square tents of translucent fabric in which you place the item to be photographed. Lights positioned outside

Photo 41. An inexpensive studio setup for static shots uses a roll of seamless paper, available from camera stores or on-line, and a pair of softboxes positioned on either side. A setup like this need not take up much space and can be broken down for storage.

the walls are filtered through the walls, creating a soft, surrounding light inside. Light cubes are available from your camera store or online at modest prices and come in a range of sizes. You can position lamps of any type outside the cube to shine through the walls to provide even lighting.

Also available are small LED light panels. These vary in characteristics. Some have adjustable brightness and the ability to vary the color temperature. Because they are small, they will be best for use as fill lights or to illuminate tiny scenes and details.

Photo 42. Norman Reid using a portable LED panel to light a scene on Mark Gionet's Boston & Maine Western Route layout.

Setting the Quantity and Quality of Lighting

If you'll be using a tripod, and you should in order to get the sharpest photos, the amount of lighting is not a big issue. If your lights are relatively bright, it'll be easier for you to work and you'll be able to use shorter time exposures and the lowest ISO sensitivity settings. However, much inexpensive lighting lacks the power of professional setups and to compensate you'll need to use longer time exposures or set your camera's ISO setting to a higher number. Be aware, however, that using a higher ISO comes at the cost of losing resolution and increasing the level of noise in your photos. We discussed ISO more fully in Chapter 3.

If you are shooting on a tripod, a more important consideration is the evenness of the lighting. Ordinarily, you'll want the lighting sources to cast smooth overhead illumination. An exception is when you want to simulate early morning or evening lighting effects, in which case directional lighting aimed from a lower level may be desirable.

As mentioned above, you should also consider the color temperature of your lighting. DSLRs and mirrorless cameras will have a light balance setting to compensate for pictures taken in bright daylight versus cloudy days or under fluorescent lights, among other conditions. Use the correct setting for your situation. The easiest way to set the light balance is using a white balance filter such as the Expo-Disk 2.0 for each change in lighting or combination of light sources. It will give you spot on color balance when shooting in Jpeg or RAW and better results than choosing the camera's auto white balance setting. If you are shooting in RAW format, you can also adjust your light balance in post-processing, but it will save time to get it right before the shot. No matter the source of lighting you use, limit yourself to only one type of lighting in any situation. Cameras can't adapt to lighting with a mixture of color temperatures and will yield unpredictable and often undesirable results when lighting such as fluorescent and incandescent lights, for example, are mixed.

In lighting your scenes, you'll generally want light that's calibrated to a daylight color temperature, unless you are trying to create a special effect. Most commercially available lights will be specified as daylight-balanced, which means they have a color temperature of about 5000 as measured on the Kelvin scale. Ordinary incandescent light bulbs, by contrast, often emit light at about 3500 K, which is why they appear yellow. The color of the light source you use is especially important if you'll be shooting in jpeg format, since your photos will reflect the color of the lighting at the time of shooting. If, on the other hand, your camera is on the RAW setting, you'll be able to adjust the color temperature later in post-processing. Most smartphones and point-and-shoot cameras don't offer the option to shoot in RAW, so you may need to be alert for light color when using them. Smartphones do have the capability to automatically adjust for variations in color balance. This is a standard feature in iPhones, but it may require third-party apps for Android phones.

> If you're shooting in jpeg mode, you'll need to pay careful attention to the light balance setting on your camera. If shooting in RAW mode, you can adjust the color temperature in post-processing.

Pay attention to the color temperature of mixed sources of lighting. Two cases where this can be problematic are with room lights and lights used with photo cubes. If the room lights are either incandescent or fluorescent bulbs that aren't daylight-balanced, they'll cause a different color on the scene than your daylight-balanced lights. This may not be apparent to you when looking at the scene, since our eyes are remarkably capable of balancing light sources. But the camera is less forgiving. The solution is to use only daylight-balanced lights throughout the room or to turn off the overhead fluorescent lights when photographing.

The same is true for photo cubes. If you light them with a desk lamp or other incandescent lamp, you'll get a yellow cast. If you mix light types, say a fluorescent light on one side and an incandescent lamp on the other, you'll get mixed colors.

There may be times when you'll want to use colored light, such as when simulating a sunset. Normally, however, you'll want to use consistent light sources, preferably daylight balanced.

Position Your Lights for the Effect You Want

While your goal is to fully illuminate the elements of your scene, you'll still want to establish a bit of directionality in the lighting so the effect is convincingly realistic. It's OK for some slight shadows to be visible, so long as they aren't too dark or harsh. Remember, your lights are the artificial sun lighting the scene, so position them to reflect the direction you want sunlight to fall on the scene.

Using Two-Light Setups

For still photography, the typical two-light setup has one light positioned behind or above the camera, perhaps slightly to one side, which serves as the main light illuminating the scene. A second light stationed to one side and further from the scene creates slight shadows that produce a modeling effect on your rolling stock, structures and people.

You'll need to experiment with the placement of the second, or fill, light and its effect on shadows. Both the angle from which it shines and its distance from the scene are important. The falloff in light is governed by the inverse square rule, which means that as you move the light back from the model, the level of lighting drops by the square of the distance from the subject. Small adjustments in positioning, then, can produce larger than expected changes in the relative intensity of your main and fill lights.

Another option is to position a light source, preferably a softbox, directly over the top of the scene and another light to one side, again at a slightly greater distance from the

Photo 43. A two-light setup using softboxes is an effective way to provide overall, soft illumination to your subject, in this case a diorama.

scene. This will produce a different configuration of shadowing that you may find more to your liking.

In some cases, you may also want to set your main light behind your principal subject at a high angle and then use fill lighting from the front or one side. However, this setup is more prone to create distracting reflections on shiny surfaces and you'll want to be alert for these.

Don't be afraid to experiment with lighting arrangements. Move your lights around until you get the results you want.

Softening Shadows

Reducing distracting shadows can be achieved in several ways. One option, as discussed, is to use a multiple light setup with two or more lights. While the best solution, this may be unnecessary for most purposes, however.

A second option is to use a reflector to bounce light into deeply shadowed areas. Inexpensive collapsible reflectors, known colloquially as elephant diaphragms, are available from camera stores or online. They come in a variety of sizes ranging from pocket size to very large. They also come in different colors, especially white, silver and gold, which allow you to create a color cast in your scene if desired. You can easily make your own reflector with a bit of crumpled aluminum foil stretched over a piece of cardboard or by using a piece of white foam core board.

Yet a third possibility is to paint light into shadowed areas. You can do this with a flashlight that's balanced for the color temperature of your main lights, such as an LED flashlight. With the camera set for a time exposure, move the light from the flashlight over the area you wish to lighten. It may not take long to reduce the shadows. You'll need to experiment to get the right balance of light between the overall scene and the shadowed area, but, pixels are free!

While you want to reduce the harshness of shadows, you don't necessarily want to eliminate them altogether. Shadows create a modeling effect, helping to show the three-dimensionality of your scene and enhance the appearance of realism. Shadows can also simulate a time of day.

However, you do need to be alert for shadows cast on the backdrop. A tall structure such as a grain elevator can easily shadow the backdrop and create an unrealistic look that ruins your shot. You'll need to position your lights carefully to avoid this.

> Shadows create a modeling effect, helping to show the three-dimensionality of your scene and enhance the appearance of realism.

A final option is to use a photographic technique known as HDR, which stands for High Dynamic Range. HDR involves capturing a set of images of a scene at different exposure levels so that one image photographs the shadowed areas normally and another captures the bright areas so they are not overexposed. The set of images is then combined in post-processing to generate a single image that is well-exposed throughout. Standalone programs such as Photomatrix are available for HDR processing, or it can also be accomplished in Adobe Lightroom or Photoshop. Depending on the range of brightness and shadowing in your scene, a minimum of three images spread two stops apart is recommended, though the sequence can include more shots if needed for very contrasty scenes.

Painting with Light

A way to achieve special effects is literally to paint a scene with light. This is done in a dark room using a neutrally balanced flashlight such as an LED light. With the camera on time exposure, "paint" the scene with light by shining it onto the areas you want to highlight. It's best to keep the light moving rather than let it rest on a single spot. Short time exposures of five to ten seconds may be all you'll need.

Light painting is one method for lighting a nighttime scene to supplement static lighting from street and window lights. Or, it can be used to highlight certain aspects of a scene. And it can also be used to create a nostalgic look if you are photographing trains for holiday cards or display photographs.

Because the results of light painting are uncertain, the process necessarily calls for experimentation through trial and error. Make several shots, each time assessing the results in your LCD screen until you get one or more images that satisfy you. With digital gear, this poses no issues other than the time you spend. And by the way, pixels are free.

Special Lighting Situations

Some circumstances call for alternative lighting arrangements. These include times when you'll want to freeze motion of moving objects or represent specific times of day.

Freezing Motion

In your still photos, there may be times when you want to capture moving objects by freezing them in motion. Examples are the falling leaves of autumn or downward drifting snowflakes in winter scenes. In either case, you can stop the action by using a high shutter speed. But the low level of light available from amateur lighting equipment will limit your ability to use a fast shutter speed without severely affecting picture quality from setting a very high ISO.

Here's a situation where a flash can be helpful. Because the duration of a flash is very short, it's capable of freezing motion in moving objects like artificial snowflakes. The challenge will be to fill shadows created by the flash so they aren't too harsh.

In this case, a multiple exposure may be helpful. If your camera has multiple exposure capability, make one photo of the scene using standard overall lighting as discussed earlier. Then make a second exposure on the same frame using flash while the snow or leaves are falling. Because you'll be doubling the lighting, you'll need to reduce the exposures so the scene is properly lit. This will require some experimentation and it may take many shots to get satisfactory results. The good news is, pixels are free! While this type of shot was traditionally a job for DSLRs and mirrorless cameras, smartphones also can make multiple exposures using third-party apps such as Photo

Photo 44. Although the scene is darkened, this village on Wolf Neudorfer's layout was illuminated by using a small flashlight to highlight individual areas. The effect simulates localized lighting within the village.

Blender for Android phones and Double Exposure for iPhones.

An alternative method that doesn't require a flash is to paint snowflakes or leaves on a sheet of glass and place it between the camera and the scene. The snowflakes or leaves will be rendered blurry, but this may be a good way to simulate movement.

Showing the Time of Day

You can simulate different times of day by altering the positioning and color of lighting applied to the scene. Suppose you want to show an early morning scene. Early morning light has two distinctive characteristics. The sun is low in the sky, so it strikes objects at an angle that casts long shadows. And because the light is filtered through more of the earth's atmospheric dust, it is usually warmer in tone, ranging from a deep gold in the earliest hours of sunrise to a lighter shade of yellow as the day progresses.

You can simulate morning by positioning the light to cast illumination low to the scene and lengthen the shadows. You can either use a yellowish light source such as a desk lamp, a piece of yellow acetate or a yellow filter on the lens to create the color of morning light.

Sunset scenes are the same, though often the light at sunset can appear even more golden than morning light. Note that if your layout is geographically oriented, that is, if it has a north and a south, you'll need to station your lights to shed shadows in the proper directions.

Night photos are different still. Now you'll want to darken the room and rely mainly on the lights from your layout—engine headlights, streetlamps, window lights, signals and so on. Depending on the nature of the lights, these may be mixed in light temperature. For window lights and engine headlights, incandescent lighting is appropriate. In these cases, daylight-balanced LEDs won't look realistic. To provide basic lighting for the dimmer areas in the scene, a low-powered blue light source can create a nighttime color cast. This is a set-up that may be best made with a double exposure, one for the overall effect and the second to burn in the smaller lights.

Photo 46. This model of a Deutsche Bahn (German Federal Railways) Class III locomotive is lit from overhead, simulating a mid-day photo shoot. The scene is set on Wolfgang Neudorfer's layout set in Ohnesorg, Germany. The Class III was a general all-purpose locomotive, with a maximum speed of 99 mph, built between 1974 and 1984. A total of 227 were produced.

Finally, midday sunlight is bright and comes from directly overhead, or nearly so. To represent noontime sun, position your lights directly over your models so there are few shadows and the light appears to be intense.

Lighting for Video

Lighting scenes for video can be more challenging. Depending on the nature of the

Photo 45. This nighttime scene of a roundhouse was shot on Wolfgang Neudorfer's layout. It was entirely lit by the overhead lights at the engine servicing facility.

Photo 47. This shot of Gleason's Bar simulates the soft overhead lighting of an overcast autumn day. It is set on Mark Gionet's Boston & Maine Western Route layout.

shots being made, the lighting arrangements may differ. For shots made from a fixed position, of a train emerging from a tunnel, for example, the two-light setup described above will work well.

The new small LED panel lights have a shoe on the base that will fit into the hot shoe on top of many DSLRs and mirrorless cameras. That's what they were originally designed for. However, if following a train as it moves around the layout is your objective, you'll need to provide even lighting over all the territory it crosses. A good way to do this is to position multiple softboxes around the layout so the entire scene is evenly lit.

Chapter 5 Photos for Documentation

Sometimes you'll want to photograph your trains for documentary purposes. You might want to sell them online on eBay or other places. You may also need to record your collection for insurance or estate planning purposes. Special considerations need to be taken into account when making photos for these objectives. We'll take them up in this chapter.

Making Photos for Sales

Good photos help potential buyers gain confidence in what they're bidding on. They'll help you as well by generating greater competition and, as a result, bringing higher prices.

When making photos for selling your locomotives, rolling stock or kits, it's important to show the items fully and clearly, so all their features and condition are readily visible. You'll need to make a complete series of photos showing all angles. Equally important are photos that show the condition of the model, including any defects that need to be called to the attention of buyers.

The quality of your photos is important too. The models should be well lit so key parts are not in shadow but can be clearly seen. Try to avoid using flash, which creates harsh shadows, flat details and shiny "hot spots." A soft, enveloping light is best. Ordinary room light often suffices if it's bright enough.

The photos also need to be sharp, so unless you can handhold your camera very steadily, use a tripod.

Choose a background that doesn't clash with the model. Something neutral such as a white sheet or a paper background is ideal.

You don't need a DSLR or mirrorless camera for sales photos. Smartphone photos can be quite good enough.

Photos for Insurance and Estate Documentation

Though many of us prefer to put off thinking about it, the potential loss of our

---

Good Photo Angles

A complete set of photos of model locomotives includes:

- The front, straight on and angled from each side
- Both sides
- The top
- The rear, straight on and angled from each side
- The bottom
- The box, if any
- Close-ups of key details
- Close-ups of defects, if any
- For steam locomotives, similar shots of the tender

Equivalent shots should be made of freight and passenger cars.

Kit photos should show the condition of the box and, if it has been opened, the parts should be photographed laid out.

---

collections and our eventual demise are both important considerations. A big part of planning for both insurance coverage and estate planning is documenting our investments in locomotives, rolling stock and the other valuable components of our layouts. The photographic evidence you'll need is similar, but not identical, for each of these purposes. Let's start with documentation for insurance.

Insurance Documentation

To begin with, you'll want to check your homeowner's or renter's policy to establish what coverage you have and, if necessary, increase it to an affordable and acceptable level. You'll then want to make an inventory of every component of your layout, including not only locomotives and rolling stock but also structures, figures, trackwork, electronics, books, tools and railroad collectibles.

Once you've created an inventory, make photographs of each item, showing enough detail to document your possession of the item and, especially for more valuable things, their condition. For rolling stock, it may be sufficient to make group photos of cars in boxes or arrayed in a marshalling yard. High value items, however, merit individual photos and should be recorded from several angles. When possible, also retain evidence of your layout's value by scanning or photographing receipts.

executors to sell our collections. The key difference between insurance documentation and estate planning is that while insurance coverage can include the cost of rebuilding the entire layout, much of the layout will have no value when it is broken down. Documentation for estate planning, therefore, only needs to include things that are usable after the layout itself has been dismantled and cut up. This

Photo 48. A series of photos such as this showing all angles and including the packaging makes the best sequence for advertising model railroad equipment for sale online.

To prevent possible loss of your documentary evidence, give copies to friends or post it to the cloud for safekeeping.

Estate Planning

The time will come for all of us when we are either no longer interested or able to maintain and operate our model railroads. Careful documentation will help us or our includes locomotives, rolling stock, removeable buildings, salvageable scenery items, track, switches and electronic components, as well as books and tools. But it excludes the benchwork, unless it is modularized or otherwise capable of being removed in sections without damage.

As with insurance documentation, you'll want to develop an inventory and make photographs of each item. Not only will these be helpful to executors, but they will also ease sales of the collection to buyers, especially those who purchase complete collections. Be especially careful to document valuable items such as brass locomotives and collectible kits. Don't forget to include books and any specialized tools such as lathes.

Chapter 6 Shooting Trains in Motion

Model railroad photography is no longer limited to still photos. With the advent of digital photography, videography is now widely used in a variety of settings, such as on web sites, YouTube channels, and Facebook postings. DSLRs, mirrorless cameras, and smartphones are now all video capable. The range of types of possible shots is quite wide.

The first word that comes to mind when thinking about homemade videos is seasick. We are sure everyone has seen homemade videos where the camera is swinging back and forth to keep up with the action. Children's soccer games come to mind! Control of your camera and advance planning are critical to creating videos that people will want to watch. It is impossible to show examples of good and bad videos in a printed book, but we will share some basic principles that will help to improve your videos.

Shooting from a Static Position

With the camera in a fixed position on a tripod, a variety of shots can be made. A classic shot is of the engine approaching the camera head-on. Or, you may elect to position the camera so the train passes by at an angle. Yet another is to shoot the train from the rear as it disappears into a tunnel or around the curve of a hill or mountain.

Just as with still photography, you have the choice of making your photos up close to emphasize details or to pull the camera back and show the train as it passes through a wider area of scenery.

You can also swing the camera in alignment with the train as it passes through a scene. This technique, known as panning, keeps the train in constant focus and allows the scenery in the background to change. If you are shooting with a handheld camera, such as a stabilized smartphone, you may also be able to make shots pacing the train as it passes through the countryside, just as though you were driving down the road alongside a moving locomotive. The key to successful panning and pacing videos is keeping the camera stable, so you eliminate jerking movements. This will be easier using a camera mounted on a fluid head. See Chapter 10. Neither type of shot is easy to make, though, and you'll likely need to experiment and repeat the shot many times in order to get good ones. The result may pay big dividends for your efforts. However, remember what we said about seasickness, which is a big risk with this type of shot unless it is carefully controlled.

Other Possibilities

There are other video shots to consider as well. In addition to daytime scenes, you can make videos of the train in the nighttime, perhaps as it passes the lights of a station or a lighted structure such as a factory or warehouse.

You need not limit yourself to a single train. How about capturing a meet or the drama of one train crossing a bridge while a second engine emerges beneath it?

Of course, you have some choices in setting up your shots. You may want to capture your train moving at full speed through the countryside. Or, you can choose to show it crawling through the yard at a restricted speed.

Finally, you have the option to show your trains unobstructed by surrounding buildings and other structures, or you can choose to frame your shots by having your locomotives emerging from tunnels, passing under overpasses or through signal bridges.

With all these options, the field for video photography of your layout is as exciting as it is vast.

The Mechanics of Making Videos

The principles of good videography mirror those for still photography. You'll need to define your audience and the story you want to tell, plan your shoot, identify the best locations, set up the shoot, capture the video, and assemble the video in post-processing. Your story may be something simple like having a train pass in front of the camera so your audience can count the hundred and one coal hoppers, or it may be a complex show about how you wired your layout. The difference between a still image and a video is that a video requires you to create a sequence of shots that are put together to create an overall story.

After you've defined your audience and the story you want to tell, you need to plan how you'll shoot your video. A typical video is a collection of clips showing the scenes, the action within the scenes and the intent of how you want the audience to react to the scenes. Your plan may be no more than a checklist of scenes for a simple story, or it may contain a script and detailed descriptions of the key shots within the scene.

Once you have a plan in place, it's time to think about how you'll shoot your scenes. If you watch professional movies or commercials, you'll notice that the overall movie is made up of short clips rather than one long continuous shot. So, think in terms of short shots. For example, if you are going to shoot a train traversing a segment of your layout, shoot the train entering the scene, then cut to the train going around a curve, and finally cut to the train leaving this segment of your layout. Short action clips tend to hold the interest of your audience better. And remember that seasick thing! Resist the temptation to shoot the train entering the scene and then move and zoom the camera to follow it as it traverses the layout.

Here are some tips for creating good videos. First, keep the camera as stable as possible. Let the action happen within the setup of the scene. If you must move the camera by panning as mentioned earlier, use a tripod with a fluid panning head or a stabilization system to minimize any vibrations and, most important, make no wild back and forth swings.

If your camera has a digital zoom rather than an optical zoom, don't zoom using the digital zoom capability of the camera. Digital zoom will reduce the image quality of the video. Read your camera's manual to understand its zoom methods. If you must zoom in, it's best to do that by moving the camera closer to the subject.

Keep your individual video clips short. Typical shots are 5-10 seconds long. Again, watch a TV commercial and count the length of each shot between transitions to see how professionals do it.

Keep the light behind you. Video cameras will typically focus on and meter exposure on the brightest part of a scene. Positioning the light behind your subject will throw it into shadow or silhouette and cause the camera to overexpose the scene. Having the light behind the camera will make the light fall on the subject so it will be the brightest object in the frame.

Once you've collected all your shots, it's time to edit and put them together in post-processing. We'll discuss video post-processing in Chapter 8. The unique aspect of video post-processing is called "non-linear processing." This means that you can shoot your video clips in any order, then later put them together in the sequence specified in your story plan. This also means that you can take multiple takes of a scene and choose the best one to use in your final video.

Finally, keep your video programs short. It is much more likely that your audience will remain engaged if the programs do not run too long. If the story dictates that you need to have a long video, consider breaking it up into episodes for a series.

Using Video Equipment

Video cameras have gotten small enough that it's also feasible to shoot video from the train as it passes over your layout. This has two benefits. Not only can you make some exciting and realistic videos, but you can also use this method to inspect your track in places that are otherwise hidden or hard to reach.

The explosion of technologies for robotics and more recently aerial drones has miniaturized the components available for use on model trains of all scales. A recent search on Amazon for "mini video cameras" returned over 30,000 products! Mini-spy cameras or security cameras now shoot in color, with either on-board storage via SD cards or the ability to wirelessly transmit video and audio to a receiver attached to a desktop computer, laptop, tablet, or smartphone. Very small pan and tilt platforms for robotics can be adapted for use to give the feeling of a viewer turning their head when looking out a passenger car window.

Complete packaged commercial systems for model railroading are available, such as RailCam from 4Kam and Train Wireless Camera from DCCTrain, among others. General purpose cameras are available, such as the GoPro Max line of cameras from GoPro or the Cube camera line from Polaroid. There are even cameras, such as the CINONEX from Insta 360, that will record 360 degrees of video.

You have several options for positioning the camera. The classic shot is from the front of the engine, which will give you the engineer's view of the scenery as the train passes through it. Cameras can be mounted on the front of the locomotive or, for the innovative, can be disassembled and the lens and sensor mounted behind the headlight, with the camera electronics in the tender or a boxcar behind the locomotive.

Also consider aiming the camera to one side. If you do, you can capture a view of the passing scenery as though you were a passenger on the train. You'll want to aim the camera away from the aisle so you are filming scenery and not the photographer and lighting setup.

Finally, with the camera stationed on the last car and pointed rearward, you can video the scenery as the train pulls away from it, the view a passenger might witness from the platform of an observation car or the conductor from a caboose.

There are a few issues to keep in mind when positioning your camera on the train. First, a camera lens does not move like your head and eyes do when sitting in a train. As a passenger looking out the side of the train window you can swivel your head and eyes. Therefore, position the camera facing slightly forward so you don't get a static sideways view. Remember that seasick thing!

Audio is also problematic. These cameras have built in audio, which is nice to capture the train whistle or bell. However, they're very susceptible to picking up track noise. It may be better to capture video with no audio, then insert audio later in post processing.

Chapter 7 Backdrop Photographs

When you create a backdrop behind your layout, you have several options. The simplest is to paint the wall or backdrop material such as Masonite a light sky blue. Many model railroaders have opted to take it a step further and decorate the backdrop by adding clouds, mountains, trees and other images of terrain. Our backdrop even features a hot air balloon! But a third option is to use photographs of actual locations. Not only will this create a realistic effect, but it may also be the easiest way to show details if you believe you aren't sufficiently artistic to paint them.

Shooting Panoramas

Making a panorama composed of a series of individual photos is the most effective way to create a photographic backdrop. To do this, take a sequence of photos as parallel as possible to the horizon. This can be done with the camera handheld, though it's easier to steady the camera on a tripod to keep it level. Shoot with the camera in the portrait position so you capture as much sky as possible in each image. Overlap the images by about a third. If you shoot several sequences—and this is a good idea to help assure you have one that works well—separate them by taking a photo of your hand before and after each set.

The greatest difficulty may lie in finding a suitable location for your panorama. Usually, you'll want to locate a site with natural surroundings unobstructed by buildings, telephone poles, utility lines and the like.

Printing Backdrops

You have two choices for printing your backdrops. You can make individual prints or you can print a panorama on a long roll of paper.

Individual Prints

This is the simplest method and the one you'll need to use if your printer lacks continuous roll paper capability. Print each image in portrait mode using the largest paper you've got. Many printers are capable of printing on 11x17 or 13x19 paper, which will give a reasonable height to the backdrop. You may find that

Photo 49.. Jeff Fleisher is preparing to photograph a diorama against the painted backdrop on the North Fork & Crooked Run Railway, our layout. The backdrop, including the hot air balloon at right, was painted by Rachel Shumway.

Photo 50. This panorama, shot in Ten Sleep Canyon, Wyoming, is one we've used as a background for shots with a diorama. The unobstructed view works well as a background for model railroad photography.

45

matte paper gives the best look by avoiding the unrealistic sheen of glossy paper.

Continuous Rolls

If your printer can accept continuous rolls, this is the preferable method. Starting with a sequence of photos you've made, you can easily stitch them together in Adobe Lightroom or Photoshop, which will eliminate the overlap between the images and create a seamless panorama that can then be printed on continuous roll paper. Again, choose matte rather than glossy paper for the best appearance.

MOUNTING BACKDROPS

To mount individual prints, you'll want to trim off any white borders, then match the prints so they line up precisely. Attach them to supporting material like foam core board or Masonite. Continuous roll prints don't require trimming or matching up since this is done electronically. Attach them to supporting material in the same way as individual prints.

In either case, you'll get the best effect by mounting them so foreground objects in the photos are kept low, letting the sky become the principal element. Then, place your models in front of the backdrop in a way that blends the backdrop into the scene.

Chapter 8 Post-Processing

The final stage of converting the photos you've made into usable forms is post-processing. You need to know several things in order to get the best results. We'll take them up in this chapter.

Calibrate Your Monitor

To get prints that match your expectations, based on the editing you've done looking at your monitor, your monitor and printer need to talk to each other accurately. To assure this, you'll want to calibrate your monitor so what you are seeing on the screen is what the computer is recording. Then, if you'll be printing your photos, you'll want to be certain that your printer is set to print correctly on the paper you've chosen to use.

To set your monitor so it's accurate, you'll need a calibration meter. These are small devices that are suspended in the middle of your monitor and connect to the computer via a powered usb port. They take readings of the color and gamma (light) values of the monitor and regulate them so they're accurate.

Two leading brands are the Datacolor Spyder5Pro and the X-Rite ColorMunki Display, which sell for $150-170. These systems offer all the capability you're likely to need. In addition to these, more advanced systems from these makers offer more user-customizability for only a little added cost.

Because your monitor will lose its calibration over time, it's recommended that you recalibrate it three or four times a year at a minimum, though arguments can be made for doing it as often as monthly. Purists and professionals concerned with absolute accuracy in their prints may calibrate as often as weekly or even daily.

The calibration process is technical and therefore little understood by average users, so it can seem daunting and is often ignored altogether in the hope that what you don't know won't hurt you. For photographers who care about the quality of their photos, this can be a big mistake. Besides, the calibration systems mentioned are easy to use and it's not necessary to understand the underlying science to get good results.

> Calibrating your monitor is technical and can seem daunting. But with the right software, the process is painless, and it can help you get the most accurate results from your model photography.

We use the X-Rite i1Profiler system, which offers two modes for calibrating a monitor. The basic mode is the simplest to use. Most of the needed parameters are set automatically. It's advised that you let your monitor warm up for 30 minutes before calibrating so the colors are stable. You then suspend the calibration device in the center of the monitor and start the calibration program. If your monitor has controls to set the contrast and brightness, you'll be given an opportunity to make those adjustments. If not, you can tell the program to skip them. The program will flash a sequence of colors on the screen, which the measurement device reads and uses to create a color profile for your monitor. When the process is complete, name your profile and save it. It's best to include the date in the profile name so you can tell which is the most recent.

The advanced mode differs by offering several adjustments not available in the basic mode, including the option to use a much larger number of color test patches to set the monitor for subtle color variations.

The X-Rite i1Profiler system also allows measurements of the ambient lighting conditions and it can adjust the profile for the effect that changes in the lighting may have on the appearance of color on your screen.

Set Up Your Paper

If you plan to print your photos, you'll also need to attend to your printer's calibration. Print papers absorb ink differently based on their inherent characteristics. To get the best, most reproduceable results, you'll need to tell your printer what paper you're using so it knows how to apply the ink to get the proper tones. If you are using a paper made by your printer's manufacturer, you'll find most of the paper choices you'll need in the print menu. But if you've elected to use a third-party paper, and there are many good ones available, you'll need to use ICC profiles to tell the printer how to treat the paper.

> If you're using your printer's proprietary paper, you can manage print settings from your printer and get great results. But if using a third-party paper, you'll be better off using ICC profiles to tell the printer how to treat the paper. These profiles can be downloaded from the paper manufacturer's web site.

ICC stands for the International Color Consortium, which was formed by eight vendors to create an open, vendor-neutral color management system that would operate over all operating systems and software packages. ICC profiles are sets of computer code that characterize a color input or output device according to standards set forth by the Consortium. The profiles are developed by paper manufacturers to coordinate their papers' performance with specific printer models. ICC profiles are downloadable from the paper makers' websites. You need to install them on your computer in order to use them.

On the paper manufacturer's web site, locate the paper you'll be using. Then, locate your specific printer model. If it's a recent printer, there should be an ICC profile for it. If not, you can create your own or have one created for you. After downloading, install it on your computer. There are generally instructions on the paper manufacturers' web sites for installing ICC profiles. Once installed, the profiles will show up in the listing of profile options when you are ready to print.

Note that the major printer makers provide ICC profiles for their own printers but not their competitors. Therefore, if you plan to use Epson's extensive line of papers on a Canon printer, for example, you'll need to choose the Canon standard print profile that appears closest to the Epson paper.

Like calibration, using ICC profiles can seem like a daunting or excessively picky exercise. But failing to use them when appropriate is guaranteed to lead to discrepancies between what you thought you were creating on the monitor and what you get in your final prints. For the best, most consistent results, you'll want to apply the proper profiles for your printer and the paper on which you're printing.

Editing Software

Several software options are available to you for editing your model railroad photos. Adobe Lightroom is probably the simplest to use and it may be all you'll ever need. Not only does it contain an array of photo editing capabilities in its Develop module, but its Library module will help you organize and keep track of your photo collection. In addition, it has modules for printing your photos and posting them to the web.

Figure 7 shows Lightroom's Library module. The left-hand panel shows the folders included in your catalog and enables you to create special collections of photos for easy access. The right-hand panel displays a histogram of your image, as well as boxes in which you can enter keywords and other metadata to identify your photo. Within the Library module you can search photos by filename or keyword. You can display the images in a small size to review and select them or at full-size as shown in Figure 7. A filmstrip view appears along the bottom edge from which you can also choose the photos you wish to view. The Library module is where you review your images to identify those you wish to flag as keepers or mark for deletion, as well as to classify them with star ratings or color codes to distinguish

Figure 7. The Adobe Lightroom Library module screen, where you can manage your collection of photos, add keywords and other metadata, code your photos for quality and other selection factors, and group photographs into "collections" for easy retrieval.

them. It's also the place from which you can export your finished photos from RAW to jpeg or other formats.

Figure 8 displays the Lightroom Develop module. Like the traditional wet darkroom, this digital darkroom provides you with an array of tools you can use to edit and make adjustments to your photos. These include cropping, changing the exposure levels, adjusting contrast, reducing highlights and lightening shadows, for instance, as well as adding texture and improving the vibrancy of your photos. You can also, if you choose, convert your color images to black & white from within the Develop module. You'll find the Develop module to be a full-featured set of tools that may be all you'll ever require.

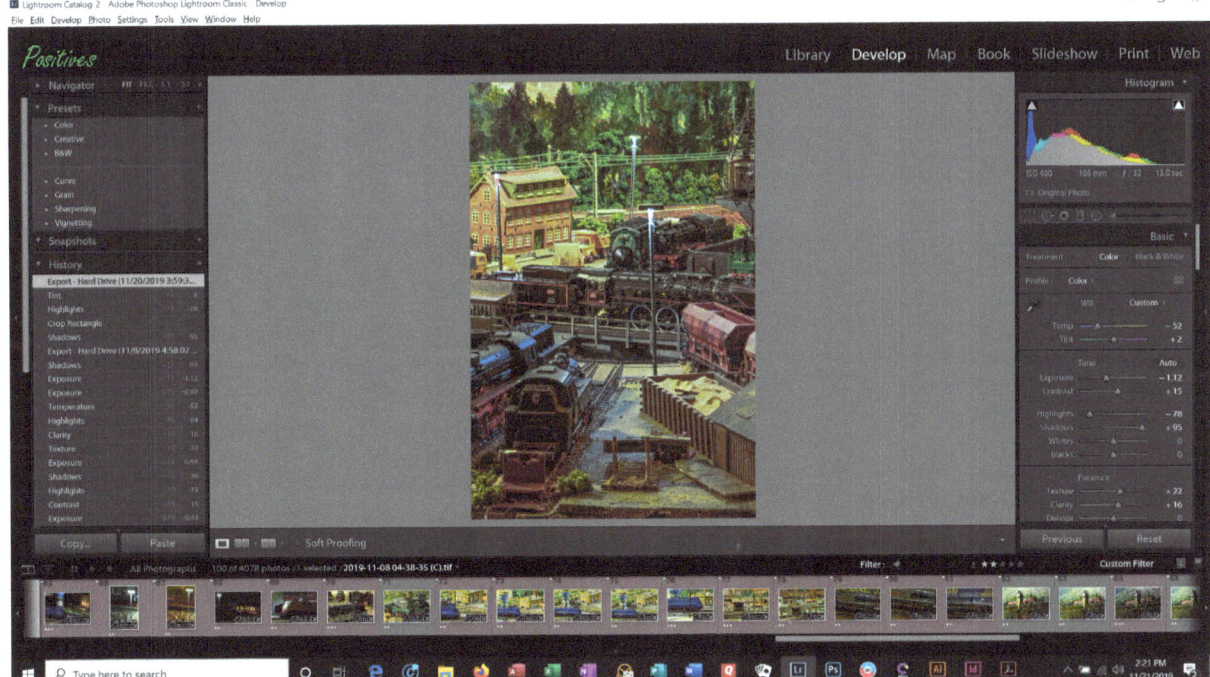

Figure 8. Lightroom's Develop module offers you several controls on the righthand panel that are used to edit photos for exposure, contrast, highlights, shadows, texture and clarity, among other elements. Its slider format makes editing straightforward.

Despite Lightroom's capabilities, there are times when you may need to do editing that employs more sophisticated techniques. When that's the case, programs such as Adobe Photoshop, Luminar, or On1 Photo Raw may be helpful. Each of these gives you the ability to use layers and apply masking to achieve special effects. An example is simulating locomotive smoke to achieve a more realistic look.

Besides these programs, others such as Paint Shop Pro may meet your needs. Some shareware programs may also work well at a very affordable cost.

Focus Stacking Photos

The simplest way to process a stack of photos made at different focal points, as discussed in Chapter 3, is to use a program such as Helicon Focus or Zerene Stacker. From Lightroom, select the photos to be stacked and export them to the stacking program. Then select a rendering method and render the stack to produce a single image.

Sometimes, the stacked photos will have unwanted artifacts such as fringing or halos. In this case, re-render the stack using a different rendering method. If the artifacts still remain, you can edit them using the software's tools or in another program like Photoshop.

Special Post-Processing Issues

Because of the restricted space in which most model layouts exist, it's common to face certain challenges to creating realistic-looking photos. One problem occurs when a part of the fascia injects itself into a corner of a photo. A similar situation is when a door, window or ceiling corner appears at the top of the photo.

One solution, as suggested earlier, is to create a temporary foreground module that can be positioned to cover the fascia or a temporary background to hide the unwanted intrusions in the sky. Another is to use the power of the editing software to eliminate the objectionable features by painting over or cloning out what's not wanted. It's also possible to substitute entirely new backgrounds electronically using the powerful masking functions of Photoshop or other software such as Luminar.

Processing Video

As with still photography, many software packages are available to edit video into a final show. Most if not all the editors are "non-linear video editors." This means that the final show can be built up from many video clips, all taken at different times and in any order, and put into a final logical sequence. These programs will have folders to store your raw video clips, supporting still images and audio files such as music files. They will also have libraries of transitions, sound effects, royalty free music clips and music generators, title slide formats, background and frame templates, plus much more to make composing your video easy yet professional looking.

We use a product called Pinnacle Studio Ultimate, which is an affordable yet powerful video editor. It will import a wide variety of photo and video formats and music file formats. It can create video output files in numerous formats as well, including popular mov, mp4, avi, and flash, among others, at high resolutions such as 1080p. Newer versions of these editors are even supporting the new very high-resolution formats. Pinnacle is representative of most video editors.

The core of an editor is its Edit module which, for Pinnacle, is shown in Figure 9. Though at first glance this screen may look very complicated, in fact it is straightforward to use. The upper left quadrant displays your folder and libraries. In this example, there is one video file in the library. The upper right quadrant shows a preview of the show at a specific point in time. It is controlled just like a DVD player, with forward, reverse, play and stop buttons. The bottom is where the tracks that hold your active media clips are located. For Pinnacle, you can see green clips, which are title slides, tan clips which are audio clips

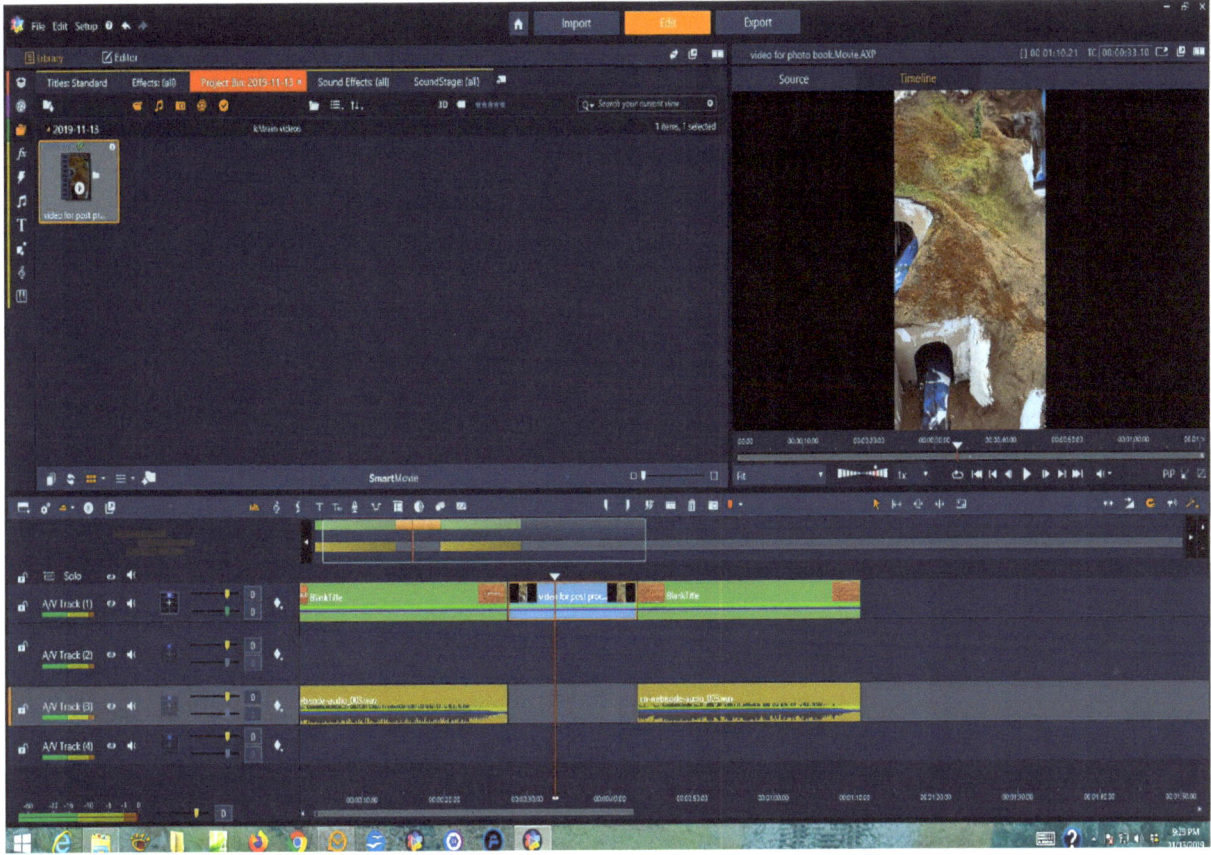

Figure 9. The Pinnacle Edit module screen.

such as music, and blue clips which are the video clips. To the left of the clips are the track labels and audio controls for each track. The program gives you complete control over the ordering of the media, and when they are displayed in the show, the overlay of one type of media onto another, and association of music or other audio with a video clip. You can even cut and paste video just like you do when editing text in a text document. All these media types are placed onto a timeline that you can see at the bottom of the display.

With non-linear editing you can easily place your media types in any sequence. With the track, located vertically, you can overlap media types so titles and still photos can overlay video, or you can set up picture-in-picture and have one video play inside another video. Even low-cost simple video editors will have many of these features.

Once your show is built, the Export module will merge all of the media on your timeline into a final show and either save it to disk or burn a separate DVD. Some programs will have capabilities to build a DVD with menus just like commercially purchased DVDs. Pinnacle will let you select the video and audio formats and final show encoding (e.g., MPEG-4 at HD 1080p resolution). The selection of these formats is usually driven by how you want to use the final video. For instance, a video burned to a DVD for high resolution display will have different requirements than a video created for YouTube or Facebook.

The amount of post-processing is dictated by the ultimate use of the video. A short clip of a train running through a single scene can be uploaded from your phone to an email or YouTube with little or no post-processing. However, putting together a story about some more complex feature or activity related to your layout may require collecting multiple video clips and compiling your story in a video editor.

Chapter 9 Completing the Job

Throughout this book we've discussed several ways to make photos of your trains and layout. Depending on how you intend to use your photos, the processing requirements will vary. In this chapter, we'll walk you through these differences and how to handle them.

Posting Photos to the Web

Processing photos for posting on Facebook, eBay, your blog or other web sites is straightforward. Often, you'll be able to take your photos right from the camera to the web.

Most cameras, including smartphones, can make photos in jpeg format. This is the most appropriate format for use on the internet because jpeg files are usually the most compact in size.

When outputting your photos, you may be given an opportunity to select a color profile for the photos. You'll want to select srbg for photos intended for the web. Srbg files reproduce more faithfully on computer screens than other color profiles.

> If you're going to post your photos to the web, choose the srbg profile, which reproduces more faithfully on computer screens than other color profiles.

Another consideration is the resolution of your photos. When creating or posting jpeg images, you'll usually be given a chance to specify the size of the photo in dots per inch, or dpi. What you choose will determine the size of the photo as it appears on the computer screen. For many applications such as Facebook, a low resolution such as 72 dpi is quite sufficient, given the small images needed. For eBay, larger file sizes will give higher resolution as well as larger photos and you may want to output those photos at something like 150 dpi. For blogs and web pages, higher resolution such as 240 dpi will allow the photos to be even larger on the screen and to be enlarged by viewers if the application enables this feature.

Prints for Contests or Displays

If you are making prints, your first decision is what type and size of paper to use. You have many choices among papers. What you decide will be governed by how you want to use the print and the look you want to achieve. For contests and displays at model railroad conferences, glossy paper reproduces well and is a good choice. If your intention is to produce photo art for hanging on the wall, you may prefer a paper with matte finish, which will soften the tones in your print and give it a more artistic look.

You also have many choices of paper size. For contests, 8½x11 paper is appropriate. For displays, larger sizes will show better. Depending on your printer's capability, 11x17, 13x19 and 17x22 are all possible. If your photograph is a panorama, you can either piece together individual smaller prints or use continuous roll paper if your printer can handle it.

Once the paper size has been determined, you'll need to size your image to fit the paper. In Photoshop, you need to first set the size of your photo. Do this by selecting Image »Image Size, then setting the width and height using inches. This works best if you are reducing the original size of your picture; although you can increase the size of a smaller original, some loss of quality can be expected if you do.

After changing the size of your photo, open the Print dialog and select your printer. Open Print Settings to be certain the photo is set to print on the proper paper size and that the correct paper type is set.

In Lightroom, select the Print module from the menu at the top of the screen. Then open the Template Browser on the left panel and select a standard print size from Lightroom's presets. If you don't find what you need, select Page Setup and open your printer's dialog to set the size and other characteristics for your print, such as paper type, print quality, and color profile. The features of the dialog box will vary with each printer model.

You'll also want to sharpen your photo before outputting it for printing. In Lightroom, this is built into the Print module. Scroll down the menu on the right, select Print Sharpening, then choose the desired level of sharpening and the type of paper, whether glossy or matte. Lightroom will handle the rest for you.

Photoshop offers more options and thus is more complicated. Open Filter»Sharpen. You then have several choices. The traditional method is to use Unsharp Mask, then set the Amount, Radius, and Threshold while watching the effect of your choices on the screen. Other automatically applied choices are Sharpen, Sharpen Edges, Sharpen More, and Smart Sharpen. You'll need to experiment to see which gives you the desired results. While some sharpening is helpful to make your photos pop, you don't want to overdo it, so in Photoshop especially, proceed cautiously.

After you have an image ready to print, you next need to decide whether to let the printer's dialog handle the printing process or manage it through Photoshop or Lightroom. If you're using a paper made by your printer's manufacturer, you can safely choose to let the printer manage the process. Select the type of paper you're using from the pulldown list of paper types offered, then, follow the on-screen instructions, paying close attention to the various parameters, especially paper size and portrait or landscape orientation. We find it helpful to enable the Print Preview function, which shows the image in miniature before it is finally printed. This has saved us from many mistakes in print size and orientation!

You can also elect to have Lightroom or Photoshop manage the print process. When you do so, you'll need to select the correct ICC profile for your paper and printer combination from among the profiles you've already downloaded and installed. You'll be given an opportunity to select black point compensation; choose it. And you'll be able to select perceptual intent. Relative Colormetric or Perceptual are good choices.

Photoshop only offers you the opportunity to make a single size print at one time. Lightroom, on the other hand, gives you much more flexibility, so much so in fact that your choices can be confusing. You can print a grid of pictures in less than page size, pairs of photos or single photos. You can combine several different photos on a single sheet. You can add borders and change the size of your margins.

From the Print menu in Lightroom, you can view your photo on the size paper you've chosen in order to see the margins and positioning. If needed, adjust the margins, decide whether you want a stroke around the photo's border, and select other options including a watermark and file information. Finally, decide whether you'll apply the ICC paper profile or let the printer determine the color matching.

Of course, if you want to sidestep this procedure or if you don't own a good color inkjet printer, you can get quality results from your local camera shop or from many pharmacies or Wal-Mart.

Photos for Newsletters

Many model railroad clubs and organizations produce newsletters, and editors are always hungry for fresh photos to share with their members. Since most club newsletters are printed in black and white (B&W), you may need to convert your photos to B&W. The exceptions are newsletters produced for online distribution. In this case, they will usually want color photos.

There are several methods for converting photos to B&W. Some cameras have a black and white mode and when this is used the original photos can be made without color. Better quality is attained, however, when color originals are converted to B&W in post-processing. Some programs capable of making quality B&W conversions are listed in the sidebar on the next page.

For newsletter production, jpeg files are fine, since they can readily be incorporated into desktop publishing programs and require minimal file sizes. In choosing file resolution, opt for higher dpi counts than for internet publication. A resolution of 240 dpi with the photo sized for its intended space, whether full or partial page, is a good choice.

Newsletter photos should be sharpened moderately for output on the type of paper, matte or glossy, that will be used. Because many newsletters are photocopied, you'll probably want to lower the contrast and increase the brightness slightly, so details are not lost in darkness in the printed copy.

Color photos for on-line newsletters can be produced in the same manner as photos intended for eBay or Facebook, except that they should be given higher resolution.

Photos for Presentations

For overhead projection, you'll want to output your photos in srbg format, which will show best on the screen. Jpeg files are quite acceptable and will take up the least disk size, though if your presentation program permits it, other formats such as gif and tiff may work as well. Because the photos will be shown on a relatively large screen, they should be displayed as high-resolution files, at least 240 dpi. The photos should also be sharpened somewhat for output to a screen.

Photos for Publication

When the intended use is publication in magazines or books, the qualitative standards are much higher. First, you'll need to output the photos in a format that has a wide gamut, or array of color reproduction. Programs such as Lightroom and Photoshop allow choices of color profiles. The widest gamut, that is, the broadest array of colors, is offered by the ProPhoto profile, and it's the best choice for publication, though the Adobe RGB profile is also good and widely used.

B&W Conversion Software

Several good programs are available to convert your photos from color to B&W for newsletters and other purposes. Photoshop and its sister program, Photoshop Elements, can do the job, though easier methods are available. These include, among others:

- Adobe Lightroom
- Nik Silver Efex Pro
- On1 Photo Raw
- Topaz B&W Effects

Files for publication can be jpeg files, but they need to be high resolution. Typically, editors want photos sized at 300 dpi at full page dimensions. This ensures that the photo will have good detail at whatever size it's used in the final publication. Sharpening for output should be modest and some editors may prefer that the photos not be sharpened at all. Smartphone photos, while they may be acceptable for newsletters, are not yet sufficiently sharp for publication in magazines or books.

Most publications have their own photographic requirements, and if you intend to submit photos for publication, you should contact the editor to obtain the magazine's photographic guidelines. Often, these can be found on the magazine's web site. Photos intended for magazine covers should be shot in portrait orientation, including some extra space around the edges to allow for cropping, and contain some relatively unoccupied space at the top of the frame so the masthead won't obscure meaningful content.

If you're photographing for publication, you'll need high resolution photos, usually 300 dpi at full page dimensions. But check the publication's guidelines; many publications have specific requirements you must meet.

Videos for the Web

The advent of smartphones with built-in video has caused an explosion of videos for the web. Taking a short video with your phone and then attaching it to an email or text message or uploading it to Facebook or YouTube has become the new normal. If you take a video that doesn't require any post-processing, using any of these services is extremely easy. Attaching a video to an email or text message is exactly the same as attaching a photograph. You will need an account on Facebook or YouTube to post to these services. Accounts are free, but you do need to use these social media services at your own risk. Your posts will not only be visible to your friends but may also be visible to others if your friends share your posts. Be aware that you lose control over who sees and uses your photographs and videos once they are posted to the web.

Posting videos on Facebook is as simple as starting a new post and clicking on the Photo/Video button. You will be directed to attach as many videos as you like and you can even add captions and location information. Once you make your selection and click on the Post button, the Facebook service will take the videos and process them to a common format and post them to the Facebook page.

YouTube also requires an account and you can use a Google account for this purpose. You can create a channel, which is a collection of videos that you've posted. You can create playlists, just as you do with music, to group your videos by topic, and you can invite others to watch videos in your channel. There are too many features to describe here, but the use and storage of your videos on YouTube is free and viewers of your channel can subscribe so they are notified whenever you add more content to your channel.

Chapter 10 Gearing Up

Of course, you'll need some gear to photograph your model railroad. In this section, we'll walk you through what you'll need to consider and offer some guidance on what to get for the kinds of photography you plan to do.

Choosing a Camera

Your journey into the world of model railroad photography will take you into a specialized branch known as close-up or macro-photography. You'll need a camera with the ability to make photos of miniature subjects. For this, you have many choices.

Digital cameras, whether Digital Single Lens Reflex (DSLR), mirrorless, point-and-shoot or smartphones, now dominate the field of photography. They have several important advantages. First, you can immediately see the images you've created. This lets you make corrections to your composition or exposure and see the improvement while you are still on the scene. Second, pixels are free and compared with film photography they cut the cost of making images to zero. Third, many camera models incorporate a feature called Live View that lets you see and compose your image on the camera's LCD screen on the back of the camera. You can see precisely what the photo will look like, both in composition and depth of field, before you press the shutter. Finally, most modern digital cameras are now able to produce videos, some with very high resolution.

If you've been photographing for very long, the chances are you already possess a digital camera. Still, it's important to know what kind of camera will best produce photos that meet your individual needs.

Smartphones

Increasingly, smartphones are being used for all manner of photography, and recent advances have made them growing favorites for close-up and macrophotography. The latest models rival DSLRs with resolution as high as 20 megapixels. Several manufacturers offer specialized close-up lenses for both Android and iPhones capable of magnifications as high as 21X! Even without such supplementary lenses, however, smartphones are quite capable of good close-up photography due to their very short focal lengths. And with special apps, some phones are now even capable of focus stacking.

Photo 51. Smart phones, like this iPhone, can make very high-quality photographs and are increasingly used for close-up and macro photography. However, they are not yet capable of creating publication quality photos for magazines or books.

Smartphones are great for publication on the web, including video clips. But the lenses in smartphones, though increasingly sharp, can't compare with the prime macro lenses used in DSLRs and mirrorless cameras. As a result, smartphones are not your best choice if your objective is high end applications like making photos for publication.

Point and Shoot Cameras

Many photographers, especially those just starting on their photographic journey, own small-bodied, single lens cameras popularly known as point-and-shoot. Sometimes, these cameras have a single fixed focal point lens, but more often they feature a zoom lens with both wide angle and telephoto capabilities.

Photo 52. Point-and-shoot cameras, such as this Leica D-Lux 6, often have sharp lenses and are capable of making high quality macro photos.

While they don't offer the same quality as DSLRs or mirrorless cameras, point-and-shoot cameras are nonetheless able to take surprisingly good images. The short focal length of their lenses makes them especially good at making close-up images. Many also offer rotating LCD screens, which are helpful for making photos in the awkward positions often necessary in model railroad photography. And their small size makes it easier to position them in awkward spots that would otherwise be impossible to reach with larger cameras.

Typically, point-and-shoot cameras have different settings, indicated by symbols, for the type of photo you want to make. Often, for close-up photography, the symbol will be a flower. When you rotate the lens ring to that setting, the camera enters close-up mode and you can then move in tight to your model scene and focus at short range.

Many point-and-shoot cameras now offer sensors in the 10-20-megapixel range, bringing them close to DSLRs and mirrorless cameras in terms of sensor capacity. The downside to point-and-shoot cameras comes in the inability to customize lens selection, the generally lower resolving power of the lenses themselves, and the fact that their zoom capabilities rely on digital rather than optical methods, which results in a loss of quality, as discussed earlier. Despite these limitations, however, point-and-shoot cameras may make excellent cameras for model railroad photographers whose goals do not extend to magazine or book publication.

DSLRs

If publication is your objective, you'll find that DSLRs and mirrorless cameras have significant benefits. Their primary advantage over smartphones and point-and-shoot cameras is the range of high-quality interchangeable lenses available for them. This lets you choose a lens that best fits making close-up photos. The major camera manufacturers offer specialized macro lenses in differing focal lengths that let you make photos at varying degrees of closeness to your subject. Canon and Nikon are the premier makers of DSLRs, but others, including Leica, Sigma and Sony, also make high quality DSLRs.

Photo 53. This Nikon D810 is a full-frame or FX camera body with a resolution of 36.3 megapixels.

FX vs. DX

DSLRs come in two main flavors, designated FX and DX. These designations refer to the size of the sensor embedded in the camera's body. FX camera bodies are "full frame," which means the sensors measure 24mm x 36mm, the same dimensions as older 35mm negatives and transparencies. DX cameras, on the other hand, employ smaller APS-C sensors to capture the same images at about 16mm x 24mm.

While both types of cameras can make high quality images of identical subjects, there is an important difference between them. Because DX sensors are cropped to a smaller size, which varies among manufacturers, there is a "crop factor" that's applied to the lens. The crop factor makes the lens behave as though it has more of a telephoto effect. For example, the crop factor for a Nikon DX camera is 1.5, which means that a 50mm lens behaves like a 75mm lens would on an FX camera, which has no crop factor. As a result, a DX camera body focuses closer, giving you a little more working distance from your subject.

Your choice of FX vs. DX also affects your lens choices. Because FX sensors are larger, they need lenses able to fill the entire sensor with a quality image. Thus, if you choose an FX camera body like Nikon's D810, you also must buy FX-capable lenses. DX camera owners have it easier. Not only do DX lenses cost less and weigh less than FX lenses, but FX lenses will also work with DX cameras. The reverse is not true, however; if you own an FX camera, then you must use FX lenses.

How important is the FX-DX choice to image quality? Not very important, as it turns out. The latest versions of both cameras can make outstanding images that are readily turned into prints as large as 16 x 20" or larger if you so choose. Thus, you can safely base your decision on other factors, such as the weight you want to carry and the amount you want to spend.

> How important is the FX-DX choice to image quality? Not very important, as it turns out. The latest versions of both cameras can make outstanding images.

Why, then, might you consider buying an FX camera body at all? FX cameras tend to be oriented toward professional and semi-pro photographers. They are therefore likely to have more advanced features, enhanced auto-focus, and larger, higher quality sensors. But for the average photographer, this matters little and if you don't see yourself as a pro, you give up little by staying with a DX camera system.

Sensor Resolution

What about megapixels? How important is it to get a camera with a really high number of megapixels in its sensor? The simple answer is it matters up to a point, and after that it doesn't make much difference.

Megapixels refers to the number of pixels, or light-gathering points, on the camera's sensor. A megapixel is a million pixels. The more pixels, the higher the resolution the camera can capture in an image. In the early days of digital photograph, sensors of only a few megapixels were common. As sensors grew larger, so did photo resolution and, hence, picture quality increased. By the time sensors got to the 10-megapixel level, picture quality had reached the point where it could be considered excellent. Today, most DX cameras top out above 20 megapixels and FX cameras reach into the 30-50-megapixel range. This is more than sufficient to capture outstanding images with a high degree of resolution. More megapixels than that only affect the size of the prints you can make, not their quality. If you want to make further enhancements in image sharpness, you'll be better off upgrading your lenses to the best you can afford.

> Today, most DX cameras top out above 20 megapixels and FX cameras reach into the 30 to 50-megapixel range. This is more than sufficient to capture outstanding images with a high degree of resolution.

Can you have too many megapixels? In one sense, the answer is yes. The more megapixels you have, the larger the resulting image files you'll have to work with when you edit the images in post-processing. Larger files put a heavier burden on computers, and unless you have the latest and most powerful model, you may find processing to be slow. Larger files also eat up hard drive space. And they may place a substantial burden on the ability of the software to complete its job. We've experienced problems processing large numbers of large size stacked photos, for example, even when using a relatively fast computer.

Mirrorless Cameras

Mirrorless cameras are the new kid on the block and they seem to be rapidly picking up where DSLRs leave off. Given their advantages, it seems likely that they'll replace DSLRs altogether a few years down the road.

Just what's different about mirrorless cameras and what are their advantages for close-up and macro photography? Mirrorless cameras are lighter and more compact than DSLRs, especially if you choose one with a smaller sensor size. Mirrorless cameras come in several sensor sizes, ranging from full frame to the smaller APS-C to Micro Four-Thirds, so you have a range of options available, but even the largest are lighter in weight than comparable DSLRs.

Because they have no mirror, there's no mirror slap when making a photograph; this reduces vibrations that can wreak havoc on the time exposures sometimes needed when close-up photos are made. Manual focus in mirrorless cameras is said to be more accurate than with a DSLR, which is an advantage in close-up photography. In addition to the many lenses designed for mirrorless cameras, DSLR lenses can be attached with adapter rings, making the lens selection quite large.

Another advantage is in depth of field. The larger the focal length, the less depth of field you get. Since mirrorless cameras in the smaller formats, APS-C and Micro Four-Thirds, use shorter focal lengths, they can get more depth of field for any given angle of view than larger format cameras.

The larger format mirrorless cameras tend to have higher ISO capability, or light sensitivity, as well as less noise at higher ISO levels. However, the newest mirrorless cameras tout very high ISO capabilities, so this may well prove to be but a slight advantage in practice.

Should you invest in a mirrorless camera system? If you are already equipped with DSLR gear, you're probably better off sticking with it at this point in the technological curve. But if you are contemplating a new camera system, mirrorless cameras are certainly something you will want to consider.

Focus Stacking Capability

In Chapter 3, we discussed several methods for creating stacks of photos to improve depth of field in your model railroad photography. These involve changing the lens's focusing ring or moving the camera and lens progressively closer to your subject as you shoot. Recently, several camera makers have released mirorless and DSLR models that have focus stacking capability, variously called focus shifting and focus bracketing, built into them. These models include the Canon EOS RP, Nikon's Z7, Z6 and D850, Olympus OM-D, and Panasonic Lumix G95. Some smartphones can also use special apps to achieve focus stacking.

In-camera focus stacking works in a similar way to the method used by Helicon Remote, though it offers less control. In the Nikon cameras, with which we're familiar, you set the focus at the closest point you want to include in the stack, then set the number of images you want the camera to make and choose a setting that represents the distance of the interval between shots in the stack. Unlike Helicon Remote, however, you cannot set the end point for the sequence. The distance interval between shots is a number from 1 to 10, with lower numbers representing smaller intervals. While this method leaves you somewhat in the dark concerning precise settings, we've nonetheless had excellent results in model railroad photography by choosing the setting 5. We've not used the other cameras, but we assume they function in much the same way.

If you are seriously considering using focus stacking in your model railroad photographs, you may want to consider purchasing a camera body with this capability.

Film Cameras

The days of film cameras, not so far distant in the past of photography, are now largely forgotten, though not yet gone. Film is still available, but less readily than in the past. Many favorite brands, such as Kodachrome, are no longer available. Film camera bodies are still obtainable, though. Leica and Nikon offer current models, and many others are available on the used market.

Compared with digital cameras, film cameras have some serious disadvantages. Rather than seeing the results of your exposure and composition immediately, you must wait for the film to return from the lab. Newer features like Live View are not available and focus stacking is not possible. Both the cost of buying film and having it developed make film photography comparatively expensive. And post-processing must take place in a chemical, not a digital, lab. Still, some photographers prefer film because of its sensitivity to light; some films handle the extremes of lightness and darkness better than many digital cameras. However, because of the limitations of film photography and the great advantages of digital equipment, we'll assume that you've chosen to go digital as we have. For that reason, we've put our attention on digital photography throughout this book.

Video Cameras

There is a wide variety of video cameras from which to choose. Your selection will depend on the kind of videography you intend to do, whether shooting from a standing position or capturing the action from a moving train.

Static Videography

For shooting from a fixed position, you have several choices. The simplest is to use a piece of gear you probably already own, a smartphone. Quality of video production from smartphones has vastly improved over the last few years and is often sufficiently good for broadcast quality, as we have done.

To get even higher quality, many DSLRs and mirrorless cameras are capable of high resolution videos. This, too, is a piece of gear you may already own; if so, high quality videos can be created at no additional cost.

The highest quality option is a professional video camera whose sole purpose is video production. This will have the most advanced features, though it's probably unnecessary unless you intend to create professional videos.

Mobile Videography

To shoot from a moving train, you'll need to get one of the many micro video cameras now available. When mounted on the front or rear of a model railroad train, they'll enable you to simulate a ride through your scenic landscape or to inspect the condition of your rails.

Micro video cameras vary in size and shape and in choosing one you'll need to consider how you'll mount it on your train and whether it is small enough to clear tunnels and other potential obstructions.

As discussed in Chapter 6, these cameras vary in the features they offer. Desirable features include Bluetooth or WiFi transmission to your phone or tablet, the ability to store video footage on a micro SD card, sound recording capability, high resolution, and remote control, whether by voice or other commands.

As an alternative to a micro video camera, you may be able to use your smartphone for this purpose, though it will likely have fewer capabilities than a camera dedicated for this purpose.

Lenses and Lens Modifiers

No camera body alone can make images, of course, so if you're using a DSLR or mirrorless camera, you'll want at least one lens capable of making close-up photographs. There is a wide range of lenses available and several ways to modify them to be even more effective for close-up photos. Let's begin with lenses.

Lenses

A wide range of lenses can be used for close-up photography. Some are specifically designed for macrophotography. But others intended for general use can also sometimes be employed.

Macro Lenses

The number and quality of lenses available specifically for macro and close-up photography attests to their popularity among photo enthusiasts. Designated as macro lenses, they are optimized for close-up work, giving good edge-to-edge sharpness even for flat subjects. Many are capable of rendering 1:1 reproductions of subjects on the camera's sensor, meaning you can get really large images of small scenes.

Macro lenses for DSLRs are available in a wide range of focal lengths. Nikon currently offers the most extensive line of macro lenses. Canon also offers lenses for macro and close-up photography. Some third-party makers offer macro lenses for Canon and Nikon bodies, notably Sigma and Tamron. In addition to these currently-available lenses, others sold in the past can still be used with many cameras and may be available on eBay or from used equipment sellers.

Photo 54. Four of Nikon's macro lenses. From left, 55mm f/3.5, 85mm f/3.5, 105mm f/2.8, and 200mm f/4. Not shown are Nikon's 40mm and 60mm lenses.

With such a wide range of lenses available, it's fair to ask why there are so many and what the differences are. Aside from the fact that a few of the lenses are suitable only for DX camera bodies, the principal differences are the focal length and the f-stop range. Focal length is important for two reasons. First, it affects the distance from your layout you'll be able to position your camera. With a longer focal length, such as Nikon's 200mm micro lens, you can stay farther away, reducing the chances you'll inadvertently bump into the delicate details on your layout and making it less likely you'll block the light facing it.

Focal length also affects the degree to which your trains will appear to be compressed in your photos. A longer focal length will compress the subject, while a lens in the "normal" range such as 55mm or 60mm will render it without compression. Of course, DX cameras with their crop factors of 1.5 (Nikon and Sigma) and 1.6 (Canon) will add a degree of compression with any lens. Canon's 180mm lens on a Canon DX camera body, for example, would register the equivalent of a 288mm lens on an FX camera body. As a result, focal length, as well as the distance between the camera and the subject, affects the perspective with which it's rendered. This is especially the case when using wide angle lenses up close, which may distort the relationship among the elements of the scene.

> Focal length affects the degree to which the subject will appear to be compressed in your images. A longer focal length will compress the scene, while a lens in the normal range will render it more like normal eyesight.

The aperture size range also matters. Because model railroad photographers are looking for maximum sharpness throughout their images, a high f-stop number such as f/32 is desirable. High f-stop numbers represent the smallest diaphragm opening on the lens and render the greatest depth of field possible without resorting to practices such as focus stacking.

Another factor is whether the lens is image stabilized. Some lenses come equipped with this feature, which can improve your ability to get sharp photos when handholding the camera. Nikon's 105mm f/2.8 VR lens is one example. Canon and Sigma also offer image-stabilized macro lenses. If you plan to make images handheld, you may find image stabilization to be an essential feature. However, when using a tripod with an image-stabilized lens, be sure to turn it off, as the lens's internal gyroscope will create vibrations that will reduce the sharpness of your photos.

> When using an image-stabilized lens on a tripod, be sure to turn off the image stabilization to get the sharpest possible photos.

Standard Lenses

True macro lenses are considered "prime" lenses because they are fixed in focal length and many, if not most, are able to move in close to make 1:1 reproductions of the subjects being photographed. However, some manufacturers advertise certain of their zoom lenses as having "macro" capability. Strictly speaking, these lenses are not true macro lenses, but rather they are close-up lenses that come near having macro capability. Is the difference important? Do you really need a prime macro lens if you can purchase a zoom lens that will perform double duty as a zoom lens and a close-up lens? Only you can answer that question, for it depends on how close you want to photograph and the size of your budget. If you want to achieve the most highly detailed photos, you may want to invest in one or more true macro lenses. On the other hand, if close-up photography of your layout is a more occasional activity, then a macro-enabled zoom lens may more than meet your needs. Most modern lenses have close-focusing capabilities, so it's worth checking your lenses before buying.

Tilt-Shift Lenses

A specialized lens that may be useful for dedicated model railroad photographers is the tilt-shift lens. Tilt-shift lenses function much like the old-time view cameras, in that the lens can be tilted up and down or from side to side, as well as being shifted along the focal plane. While wide-angle versions of these lenses are used for architectural and landscape photography, longer focal length versions are useful for macro and close-up photography. Both Canon and Nikon make tilt-shift lenses. Nikon's longer focal length offering is an 85mm f/2.8 macro lens; Canon makes both 90mm f/2.8 and 135mm f/4 lenses. Nikon calls its tilt-shift lenses Perspective Control or PC, but it's just terminology; the functions remain the same.

In their close-up applications, tilt-shift lenses are used by tilting the lens downward toward an elongated or stretched out subject. The effect is to increase the zone of sharpness, or depth of field, in the photo. This is especially helpful, for example, when photographing a train that recedes into the distance. The tilt-shift lens can help bring both the front and rear of the train into sharper focus.

Lens Modifiers

All lenses, even macro lenses, are limited in their ability to get in close and make the biggest enlargements. To address those limitations, several types of lens modifiers are available. In general, these can be used with both true macro lenses, macro-enabled zoom lenses or other lenses.

Extension Tubes

Extension tubes are plastic or metal collars that attach between the camera body and the lens. Extension tubes contain no glass but instead are hollow extensions to the lens. By increasing the distance between the lens elements and the camera body, they increase the magnification factor and bring subjects into closer focus.

Extension tubes are made by Canon and Nikon, as well as by third-party makers to fit the major brand cameras. They come in a variety of lengths. The longer the tube, the greater the magnification effect. In addition, they can be stacked together to create even greater magnification.

The most desirable extension tubes have electronic connections that support the camera's automatic light metering and autofocus functions. Major camera brand extension tubes, as well as those made by Kenko, offer this feature. Less expensive third-party extension tubes may not offer lens coupling capabilities, so this is something to be alert for when considering a purchase. Note, however, that even tubes that are meter coupled will not record metadata with the image, so you will need to record information such as the shutter speed and f-stop manually.

The most common widths are 12mm, 20mm and 36mm, though the sizes vary among manufacturers. In addition to extension tubes of a fixed width, at least one maker, Savage, offers an extension tube that is variable, with a range of 55mm to 71mm for Nikon lenses and 40mm to 56mm for Canon lenses.

Because extension tubes increase the distance between the lens and the camera's sensor, some falloff in light occurs. This is less than would be the case when a tele-converter is used, since there is no intervening glass to absorb light as with a tele-converter. Still, the loss of light needs to be accounted for in setting the exposure. With extension tubes that are meter-coupled, this is not a problem, since the meter will adapt to the changed light levels and set the exposure accordingly. If you have non-coupled extension tubes, you will need to allow more light to reach the sensor by opening up the f-stop.

We've heard some reports of problems with autofocus functioning with third-party makers of extension tubes. While this may be annoying, in fact you are better off focusing manually when making macro photos, since this allows more precision in establishing a focal point. For that reason, problems with autofocus should give you little trouble.

To get the maximum magnification with extension tubes, set the focus on your lens to its minimum distance, then move the camera back and forth until you have the subject in sharp focus. You'll find a focusing rail, discussed below, to be helpful in achieving precision in such close focusing.

Tele-converters

Tele-converters are somewhat like extension tubes in that they fit between the camera body and lens and are intended to bring the subject into closer focus. Unlike extension tubes, however, they incorporate glass elements to modify the optical characteristics of the lens to which they are attached. Tele-converters come in three sizes, not all of which are available from all manufacturers: 1.4X, 1.7X and 2.0X. The numbers represent the extent to which the focal length of the lens is increased when the tele-converter is used. A 1.4X tele-converter would increase the effective focal length of a 200mm lens to 280mm, a 1.7X tele-converter would make it 340mm and a 2.0X tele-converter would yield a 400mm focal length.

Normally, tele-converters are used with telephoto lenses to help bring distant subjects such as wildlife into closer focus. However, there is no reason why they cannot be used in close-up photography to make small subjects appear much larger.

Several things need to be borne in mind, though. First, using a tele-converter with a telephoto lens results in a photo with limited depth of field. This means your photo will not be sharp from the front to the back of your scene.

Also, not all tele-converters are made equal. That is, some tele-converters are intended for use only on designated lenses. This is the case for Sigma's 1.4X and 2.0X tele-converters, which can only be used on their lenses. In general, for any lens you need to use a tele-converter from the same manufacturer.

Then there's the issue of light loss. Teleconverters contain glass optical elements, which absorb some of the light that passes through the lens. A 1.4X tele-converter will cost about one stop of light, while a 2.0X tele-converter absorbs two stops. The 1.7X tele-converter falls in between. As a result, you'll need to adjust your exposure when using a tele-converter, either by increasing the ISO, opening up the diaphragm or lengthening the time the shutter is open.

Tele-converters can be used in combination with extension tubes to get either greater magnification or more working distance from your subject. To maximize magnification, if you want to show a small portion of your layout in great detail, attach the extension tube to the lens and then add the tele-converter next to the camera body. On the other hand, if your goal is to give yourself more working room, reverse the sequence and attach the tele-converter to the lens first and then the extension tube to the camera body.

All things considered, tele-converters may not be your best choice for model railroad photography. However, if you already own one, it remains a viable option to consider.

Close-up Filters

Yet another option is attaching a close-up filter to the front of the lens. This is a less costly alternative to purchasing a macro lens. Good close-up filters are made of optical glass and screw into your lens's filter threads, modifying the lens to bring subjects into closer focus.

Close-up filters are widely available, many at bargain basement prices that are attractive to photographers on a limited budget. But this is one case in which you get what you pay for, or rather, you don't get what you don't pay for. The cheap filters that flood the marketplace generally yield inferior results and are best avoided if you want your close-up photos to be in sharp focus.

The best filters are achromatic lenses that incorporate two elements and are highly corrected to yield accurate results. One good set is manufactured by Canon. Canon's 500D close-up filter incorporates two glass optical elements to provide superior results. The 500D is specifically intended for use with standard telephoto lenses in the 70-300mm range. However, it has been used with success making creative close-ups even when screwed to wide angle lenses. The Canon line also includes the 250D, designed for non-macro lenses with shorter focal lengths. The Canon close-up filters are available in several sizes and screw onto the lens's filter threads, making them compatible with lenses from other makers. Century Precision Optics and Hoya also make achromatic lenses. Nikon's now-discontinued line of close-up filters are still available on eBay.

Tripods and Related Gear

Many photographers think they don't need a tripod to make a quality image. This belief comes from being able to handhold a camera when shooting landscapes where there is lots of depth of field, good lighting and relatively short exposure times. However, with close-up photography we are often dealing with just the opposite conditions: the need for high f-stops and long exposure times, very small depth-of-field, high magnification, and very precise focusing. In addition, photo composition, especially at high magnifications, can change dramatically with very small camera movements. For these reasons, a tripod must be considered essential gear for model railroad photography.

> As magnification increases, depth-of-field decreases, often to only inches or fractions of inches. Any camera movement is magnified as well, which can result in blurry photos. Tripods minimize camera movement.

Stabilizing the Camera

First, a tripod will help stabilize your camera and improve the sharpness of your photos. Model railroad photography often requires high magnification and very shallow depth-of-field. As magnification increases, depth-of-field decreases, sometimes to only inches or even fractions of an inch. Increased magnification magnifies camera movement as well and can easily produce blurry photos. To increase depth-of-field, you might want to increase your f-stop to, say, f/22 or f/32, which requires either a longer shutter speed or a higher ISO setting. Because higher ISO settings increase digital noise, the usual practice is to reduce the shutter speed. Thus, you may need exposure times of 5-10 seconds or even longer. A tripod can eliminate camera movement during these long exposure times

Aiding Composition

Tripods also help with composition. Many times, it seems we nearly stand on our heads to get the camera into a position close to the layout and then hold it at a strange angle while we compose and expose the image. A tripod lets you comfortably set up the scene, adjust the f-stop to achieve the desired depth of field, and then step back and re-examine the setup before clicking the shutter. As you move closer to the layout, magnification increases and even the slightest movement will not only blur the image but also change the composition. If you aren't careful, what was a nicely framed locomotive may lose a wheel off the edge of the frame without you even knowing it! A tripod helps assure that you end up with the photo you set out to make.

Doing Other Things

Finally, you may need to do other things while making the photo. You may need to hold a diffuser or reflector to modify the light, move a distracting element out of the way, hold a remote shutter release or position a printed background behind the subject. You may well ask, "How can I do all these things and still hold my camera to take the picture?" The tripod will come to your rescue.

Desirable Features

A good tripod needs to be sturdy enough to hold your camera and lens without tipping or flexing, especially if you have a full size DSLR camera and a long lens. Be sure that any tripod you select is rated for the load you intend to mount onto it. It should also be able to reach the levels at which you'll be shooting. If you have a shelf layout, for instance, you'll want a tripod that's tall enough to reach it.

There are many tripod configurations. Some come with a tilting and rotating center column to cantilever over your subject. These can be very useful for reaching into otherwise inaccessible spots on your layout, but use them cautiously so the extending arm does not introduce vibrations into the setup. Others have center columns that can be used to increase the camera's height. Be wary of these, as center columns reduce overall stability and can result in less than sharp photos.

What do we recommend? There are many quality tripod manufacturers such as Gitzo, Induro, Manfrotto, Really Right Stuff, and Vanguard, among others. You won't be disappointed with a tripod from any of these manufacturers. Though we recommend carbon fiber tripods for field work because of their lighter weight, this isn't much of a consideration for model railroad photography and an aluminum tripod should serve you well. We recommend a tripod with three rather than four leg sections because of ease of use and enhanced stability. Finally, though we've used tripods with short center columns for years, we're now starting to explore the newer tripods with tilting center columns. The Vanguard Alta Pro 2+ appears to be very sturdy and the flexibility the tilting center column provides in setting up close-up shots is a real plus.

Short tabletop tripods or supports such as the Kirk Low Pod are another option. These allow you to position the camera at the same level as your layout and may be convenient to use when shooting on a table or other flat surface. Tabletop tripods are available in a variety of configurations and prices.

Bean Bags as an Alternative

A bean bag is another possibility. When the camera is fired remotely, the resulting photos will be as sharp as if a tripod was used. You can easily make a bean bag by sewing fabric or leather into a pouch about eight inches square and filling it with dried beans,

Photo 55. The Kirk Low Pod offers a stable platform for close-up photography.

lentils or Styrofoam balls. Zip lock bags filled with beans also work. Bean bags are available commercially at low cost, including some that are constructed in a saddle-like configuration to fit over a sawhorse, ladder or chair back.

Photo 56. A bean bag can provide a very stable platform for photos made close to the surface. You can purchase one like this Grizzly model or easily make your own.

Gorillapods

Joby's Gorillapod is a tripod with flexible legs that can be easily positioned in many ways and can even be tightly wrapped around a ladder, chair back or other supporting structure. A Gorillapod is less stable than a rigid tripod, however, and that or a bean bag may be a better choice. But they can be an excel-

Photo 57. The Joby Gorillapod, though less stable than a rigid tripod, offers an option for stabilizing a camera in awkward situations or holding other gear such as reflectors.

lent support for auxiliary devices, such as an off-camera flash unit or to hold a reflector or diffuser.

Smartphone Tripods

Special tripods with mounting clamps to hold smartphones are useful for smartphone photography. These are generally small and can be readily positioned on a layout. Joby makes a GripTight Gorillapod Stand specifically designed to grip a smartphone. This sort of tripod, with legs that can be flexibly bent to sit in awkward positions, may be the best option. These are priced under $30.

Selfie Sticks

Selfie sticks are another option for positioning a smartphone in awkward or hard to access locations or for unusual viewpoints. The chief difficulty with selfie sticks is assuring the stability of the smartphone when held at arm's length. Stabilizers that employ gyroscopes are available to steady the smartphone and address problems of movement. Using a stabilizer, good quality photos or video of moving trains may be achievable.

Tripod Heads

The last critical element for a good tripod is the head that the camera is mounted on. The head is the part of the tripod that allows you to tilt and rotate the camera. There are many types of heads on the market, but for still photography we recommend a good ballhead. A ballhead gives you maximum flexibility when trying to set up an awkward shot. The head is typically sold separately from the tripod base. This lets you match the head and tripod to your needs. There are many heads on the market and this is another case where you get what you pay for. The most critical factor in choosing a ballhead is being able to lock down the clamping mechanism so the head doesn't drift. We have used heads where it was necessary to anticipate the drift to get the image properly composed. The tripod manufacturers mentioned earlier plus Kirk Enterprises make ballheads that are excellent for closeup photography.

There is a new ballhead on the market that may be a real game changer for close-up work. Most ballheads have a small U-shaped section in which the ball rotates to tilt downward. These ballheads are rather restrictive. A new ballhead by Acratech called the Ultimate Ballhead has the entire front section of the mount cut away, providing a full range of movement both downward and side-to-side with virtually no restrictions.

Smartphone Mounts

For smartphones, special phone mounts are available to attach your phone to a tripod. Some features we like are an Arca-Swiss type mounting plate on the bottom, sufficient size to hold a large smartphone, and a cold shoe on top to attach an LED light for added front illumination. One that has these features is the Dot Line Titan folding mount, a machined aluminum mount that costs just under $40.

Fluid Heads

If you're planning to video your layout using a DSLR or mirrorless camera, your requirements will depend on whether you're planning still shots or moving video sequences. If you won't be moving the camera and filming a train as it moves through the scene, the ballheads and smartphone mounts mentioned above will work just fine. But if your intention is to move the camera to follow a train or make a pan shot of the layout, you'll probably want to purchase a fluid head. A fluid head will allow you to move the camera with a minimum of hesitations so the filmed result is smooth. A wide variety of fluid heads are on the market. You'll need to consider the alternatives carefully to assure that your needs are met. The reviews from previous purchasers can be very helpful when deciding on a specific model.

Photo 58. The Acratech Ultimate Ballhead is capable of easily pointing the camera at 90 degrees, making it highly effective for many model railroad photography applications.

Mounting Plates and L-Brackets

One last feature to mention are mounting plates and L-brackets. These plates and brackets let you attach your camera to the tripod head using a quick release mechanism without having to screw the camera directly to the tripod. The most common are the Arca-Swiss type mounting plates. You mount a plate onto your camera or to a lens mount on larger lenses, then connect these to a mounting mechanism on the tripod head. A quick release knob or lever lets you quickly mount or unmount your camera and lens. An L-bracket is an L-shaped bracket that mounts to the bottom and side of your camera and allows your camera to be quickly mounted either horizontally or vertically to the tripod head. Other proprietary types of mounting plates are available, but Arca-Swiss is the industry standard and many other brands use this style plate as well.

Lighting Equipment

An advantage of closeup photography is that you can modify or control the lighting of your subject. Landscape photographers typically like to shoot first thing in the morning or late afternoon to take advantage of the morning sunrise or setting sun lighting. But for model railroad photography, you can shoot 24/7.

Reflectors and Diffusers

A reflector will bounce light into your scene to light shadowed areas. Most reflectors have a silver coating on one side and a gold surface on the reverse. The silver side will reflect natural lighting into your scene, while the gold surface will give a warmer look. A 12" reflector is a good size. You don't need to purchase a reflector, however. You can make your own with a sheet of white cardboard or foam core board or a piece of cardboard covered with crinkled aluminum foil.

Diffusers are screens that are used to soften the glare of harsh lights. These can be purchased inexpensively and are available in models that can be collapsed to pocket size. Some come combined with a reflector in a single package.

Portable Lights

There are times when you will need to add light to fill shadows, replicate the appearance of sunlight, or highlight a specific area. You can do this with either a handheld flash unit or the new small full spectrum LCD panels that are made for videography.

Flash

Today's compact flash units can communicate wirelessly with your camera and other flash units and can be adjusted to be either the primary light or to a low level to gently fill in shadow areas. You can still use a wired connection between the camera and flash, but we highly recommend using a camera and flash combination that supports wireless communication. The light emitted from a flash is similar to the mid-afternoon sun, with a color temperature of about 5500K (Kelvin). You can adjust the color temperature of the flash's light by adding colored gel filters.

The newer cameras and flashes work seamlessly in a commander (camera) and remote (flash) configuration. The pop-up flash on most newer cameras can be set to control one or more remote flashes. Most wireless systems use an optical communications link

Photo 59. This Nikon SB-700 flash is capble of being controlled from the camera as an off-camera unit.

between the commander and the remote. This is fine for relatively short distances such as model railroad layouts, but if you need to trigger your flash over a long distance you may want to consider radio-controlled systems. Radio-controlled systems also do not require a line-of-sight between the commander and the remote.

There is no shortage of flash manufacturers. All camera manufacturers offer a line of flash units designed to work seamlessly with their cameras, and many third-party companies have offerings as well. Because of the complexity of the electronics and the communication requirements between the camera and flash, we recommend you purchase a flash from your camera manufacturer. This will increase the likelihood that they will work together properly.

When using a flash for model railroad photography, never point the flash at the layout from the camera's position. This will create both flat lighting and unnatural-looking shadows. Instead, position the flash to one side. You'll get better results using multiple flash units. But you'll do even better by using other types of lighting, as discussed in Chapter 4.

LEDs

One issue we have with flash is the inability to see its impact until after the shot is taken. That's not as much of an issue with digital cameras, because you can instantly see your image on the camera's LCD monitor. Continuous light is a better option, though. It was less available until recently, but with the advent of LED lights things are changing.

One of the benefits of camera manufacturers putting video capabilities in DSLR cameras is that lighting manufacturers are using the new LED light technology to create small, portable full-spectrum lights that fit into the flash mount on the top of the camera. These lights, which can also be handheld or positioned on a tabletop tripod, provide continuous lighting you can see through the viewfinder. LED lights won't stop action like a flash

Photo 60. Portable LED lights like this Yongnuo YN300 are an inexpensive way to bring light to your subject, both in the studio and in the field. This model offers a choice of two light temperature levels and allows variable light levels, both desirable features that are available from a variety of makers.

will, but that is not the intent for most model railroad photography.

Most LED lights can be dimmed, and many have adjustable color temperature settings to provide both daylight and slightly warmer color temperatures. They are perfect for filling in shadows, back-lighting and side-lighting. The fact that these lights remain cool makes them ideal for dealing with temperature-sensitive subjects.

Ring Lights

Ring lights are typically used for portraiture, macrophotography and other applications that involve close-up work with only one subject. They are either made up of several small bulbs forming a circle or one circular fluorescent bulb. The ring can be small and fit right onto the front of the camera or rather large, with the camera mounted in the center of the ring. A ring light provides a diffuse light around the subject and reduces harsh shadows. In closeup and macrophotography, a ring light distributes light around the subject to fill in shadows and bring out details.

Ring lights come in a variety of configurations. Some produce a light that surrounds the lens, while others allow the decision to use

Photo 61. The Sigma ring flash is compatible with many camera brands and is mounted to the lens with a ring adapter.

light from only one side of the ring. Some offer continuous lighting, while others employ flash. Some have modeling lights. Some ring lights use LED light with varying numbers of bulbs. However, ring lights have the disadvantage of creating circular highlights in reflective subjects.

Another configuration uses side lights on flexible arms that can be positioned around the subject to create modeling light. The Nikon R1 and R1C1 systems are examples of this. Twin flash systems have the advantage of greater flexibility in use. The angle and output of the two flashes can be adjusted independently, giving greater control over the lighting. They can even be dismounted to offer side or back lighting. And they avoid the problem of circular highlights in reflections.

Softboxes

Your best bet for broad, diffused, shadow-free lighting is to use a large light source that floods the layout with soft light. For this reason, we prefer softboxes rather than floodlights or multiple flash units. Softboxes are large fabric-covered boxes that sit atop a stand positioned to light your scene from the front, side or above. They come in varying sizes, but the larger the lighting surface, the more diffuse and less directional the lighting they produce. A set of 24x24 inch softboxes will be more than adequate. You can get a set with stands for under $100. If you intend to do much model railroad photography, it will be well worth the investment.

Focusing Rails

Focusing rails are devices that fit between your camera and tripod and enable focus changes in very small increments. When you are dealing with high magnification and need to adjust either focus or composition a very small amount, you generally do not want to move the focusing ring on your camera or slide the tripod back and forth. A focusing rail lets you adjust the camera and lens position. It normally consists of two metal plates connected with a rack and pinion mechanism. One side attaches to the tripod and the other to the camera or lens mount. One knob will move the upper plate back and forth in very small increments and a second knob will lock it in place. Some focusing rails will move both back-and-forth and side-to-side. The side-to-side movement helps with composition, while the back-and-forth movement deals with focus.

Earlier we discussed focus stacking as a method to increase depth of field in your image. Focus stacking is a collection of images, each made at a different focus point in your

Photo 62. A focusing rail such as this one from Promaster enables small adjustments to the camera's position and focus both in the studio and the field. It is especially helpful for focus stacking multiple exposures.

scene, that are then merged using post-processing software on your computer. You can change the focus between shots by either rotating the focus ring on your camera or by using a focusing rail to move the camera and lens combination. There are advantages and disadvantages of each approach, as was discussed above.

Focusing rails can be very useful but, like anything, there are concerns as well. The more things you stack between your tripod and the camera, the more potential for vibration is introduced. A single direction rail will be more compact than a dual direction rail and will also be more stable. Look for a high-quality rack and pinion mechanism that moves smoothly and a rail with enough weight to help dampen vibrations.

Stackshot

A specialized type of focusing rail is the StackShot by Cognisys. StackShot is an electronically controlled macro rail system that coordinates the movement of the macro rail and the triggering of the camera. StackShot's simple user-interface makes the automation of the entire image collecting process for focus stacking very easy.

The StackShot has a rail adjustment with accuracy down to 2 microns. The system is completely configurable. You can control such features as timing (both on, off and settle), number of pictures per step (useful for

Photo 63. The Stackshot is a motorized rail system that fires a sequence of photos at specified distances from each other for focus stacking.

HDR to create an HDR focus stack), maximum speed per step, camera settle time after moving and before exposure, and much more.

The StackShot focusing rail advances the camera's position through the selected range of focus but does not change the camera's focusing ring. This method is independent of the camera and lens make and it can be used with non-autofocus lenses. It changes the perspective as the sequence of images is captured.

Helicon Remote

There are also software applications that can drive the focusing ring on many DSLRs. One such program, Helicon Remote, sets the near and far focusing points and automatically computes the focus stacking step increase for a given f-stop. When started, Helicon Remote steps to each focus location and takes exposures automatically. Helicon Remote attaches your camera by cable or Wi-Fi to an Android or IOS device and controls the focus point for compatible cameras and lenses. This method has the effect of changing the magnification of the lens as the focus ring is automatically adjusted by the software. This method requires the use of an autofocus lens.

Focus Stacking Software

Stacked photo sequences need to be processed using software designed to combine the stacked images in order to get the best depth of field possible. As discussed in Chapter 3, numerous software packages are available for this purpose, some free. The best, however, can be purchased for a modest fee. They are Helicon Focus and Zerene Stacker. Each program offers several algorithms for combining photos to get the best results. They operate by processing your stacked sequence and combining the in-focus elements so the final image represents the best from each individual photo. Both programs offer free trial downloads so you can test them before making a purchase.

In addition, Adobe Photoshop and On1 Photo Raw can be used to process stacked images. Photoshop creates a separate layer for each image. You can then use the Auto-Align layers and Auto-Blend Layers functions to render the stacked image. Once the stacked image is created you can crop and process it as usual.

74

Conclusion

As we've traveled this journey, we've seen many ways to make and use model railroad photos. The sights you've seen along the way should give you plenty of ideas about how to sharpen your artistic eye and make outstanding photos.

So, now that you know how it's done, it's time to get to work and make the photos that will show off the best of your layout!

Toot! Toot!

www.ingramcontent.com/pod-product-compliance
Lightning Source LLC
Chambersburg PA
CBHW041546220426
43665CB00002B/42